# The Author

Malcolm Wicks was the Labour Member of Parliament for Croydon North West and Croydon North from 1992 to 2012. As a government minister he was, at various times, responsible for lifelong learning, pensions, energy and science. His private member's bill, which became the 1995 Carers (Recognition and Services) Act, provided the first ever legal recognition for carers.

He also made a number of important contributions to thinking and policy around social policy, the future of the family and the role of values in politics. His publications include 'Old and Cold: hypothermia and social policy' and 'A Future for All: do we need a welfare state?'

He was married to Margaret and had three children and seven grandchildren.

# MALCOLM
# WICKS

## My Life

Matador
9 Priory Business Park,
Wistow Road, Kibworth Beauchamp,
Leicestershire. LE8 0RX
Tel: (+44) 116 279 2299
Fax: (+44) 116 279 2277
Email: books@troubador.co.uk
Web: www.troubador.co.uk/matador

ISBN 978 1783061 020

British Library Cataloguing in Publication Data.
A catalogue record for this book is available from the British Library.

Printed and bound in the UK by TJ International, Padstow, Cornwall
Typeset in 11pt Bembo by Troubador Publishing Ltd, Leicester, UK

**Matador** is an imprint of Troubador Publishing Ltd

MIX
Paper from
responsible sources
FSC
www.fsc.org   FSC® C013056

*Editor: David Utting*

# *Contents*

# *Introduction*

This volume constitutes an unusual enterprise, both in its conception and ultimate concept. To start with the latter, the book contains two parts: the autobiography of my father, Malcolm Wicks, and a collection of his essays. Yet it is the circumstances of its development that are remarkable and led directly to the actual form of this book.

Malcolm was diagnosed with terminal cancer almost one year to the day before his death in September 2012. As well as continuing his beloved profession as Labour Member of Parliament for Croydon North, he spent part of his final months writing his memoirs. His contribution across a number of fields has been recorded elsewhere, and naturally his memoirs provide his own take on these episodes. They also record, for the first time, Malcolm's hitherto unknown role in the formation of Child Benefit.

By the summer of 2012 Malcolm knew he was running out of time ('I'm up against a bit of a deadline', as he put it). He and I discussed the best way forward and decided on complementing the memoirs with a small number of his essays. There are three covering in turn, government, policy and values. They capture the range of issues that mattered most to him, including the role of values in politics, their relevance to social policy in particular and the potential for the 'contributory principle' to rejuvenate the welfare state.

The first essay, 'What Ministers Do', however, aims at a different goal – to provide some insight into ministerial life. The essay is precious here too because it helps fill a gap in the memoirs, as Malcolm was only able to provide a few sketches of his time as a government minister. Published in July 2012 in Political Quarterly, this chapter also serves as a bridge from the memoirs to the essays.

The second essay arose out of a conversation with MPs David Blunkett and Paul Goggins. They suggested, given the confluence of his recent thinking on social policy and his physical outlook, that Malcolm should give a lecture for the IPPR think tank. The result was 'Rights, Wrongs and Responsibilities: citizenship and social policy'. It was delivered at the House of Commons on 24ᵗʰ April 2012 and later published by the IPPR. Those fortunate enough to be present recall something of a reckoning and culmination of a life's work.

The third and final chapter in Part 2 centres on the role of values in politics, in particular the potential for the classic triumvirate of 'Liberty', 'Equality' and 'Fraternity' to reinvigorate the Labour Party in the years ahead. In order to apply such values to the modern world, the "bridging concept" of citizenship is proposed as a means to tackle a number of contemporary policy problems and to renew public support for the welfare state.

It is unlikely this book would have been produced in different circumstances. As such it represents a 'small secular blessing' to his friends and family. More than that, Malcolm hoped it would be read and make a contribution in the years to come.

Roger Wicks
October 2013

# Acknowledgements

Throughout the period he edited this volume, it was ever clear why Malcolm recommended David Utting for this task. We are hugely grateful to him for his time and dedication.

A real debt of thanks is also owed to a number of lifelong colleagues and friends. To Frank Field for putting to paper the powerful words first heard in his address at Malcolm's memorial service. In addition, Jonathan Bradshaw and Melanie Henwood provided support and guidance at key points in the development of this book.

Louise Szpera, Malcolm's parliamentary secretary for all his 20 years in Parliament, helped record nearly all the words to be found here. Our gratitude also goes to his constituency team – Alison Butler, Alisa Flemming and James Chalmers – for supporting him over many years.

Thank you to the photographic team comprising Tony Hall, Margaret Wicks, Caroline Oliver and Sarah Hein, and to Margaret Wicks who prepared the index.

Finally thanks go to the team at Matador.

Roger Wicks

# *Foreword*

It is entirely appropriate that the tributes paid to Malcolm Wicks since his death in September 2012 have been rich and numerous. He was a remarkable man and on many different fronts. From all that has been said and written about him it quickly becomes apparent that there was not one, but many Malcolms; such were his talents, interests, and the range of activities in which he was involved. This, his autobiography, complemented by lectures and essays, provides a welcome measure of the qualities that made him impressive in so many ways – albeit written with all the self-deprecating humour that was another of Malcolm's virtues.

Almost everyone who reads this book, even those who knew Malcolm personally, will gain new insights into his life. I can say this with confidence, knowing that the autobiography reveals one secret that until his death was known only to a tiny handful of people. The event took place in 1976 when Malcolm was a civil servant at the Home Office. What he did was to leak Cabinet Minutes of the then Labour Government concerning efforts to postpone and potentially prevent the introduction of Child Benefit.

I as the then Director of the Child Poverty Action Group (CPAG) was the fortunate recipient of the leak. So I can readily confirm that Malcolm was, indeed, the source that – with reference to the leaker in America's Watergate scandal – I referred to as 'Deep Throat'. Without the leak of Cabinet Papers, it is entirely possible that Child Benefit would never have been introduced. Malcolm ensured that some truly shameful manoeuvring within the Callaghan Cabinet to ditch one of Labour's central manifesto pledges was exposed. Through what the *Observer* newspaper went on to describe as "the most extensive leak of cabinet papers [in a] century", he also made sure the CPAG was in poll position to pressure the Government into a further U-turn to get itself back on track. The biggest-ever redistribution of income to families, and particularly poor families was thereby secured – and without Malcolm's leak none of this redistribution would have taken place.

I am unlikely to forget the political mayhem created by Malcolm giving me, as he recalled in the last months of life, his 'copious notes' made from reading the relevant Cabinet papers. I used these notes to write an article, *Killing a commitment,* which I offered to Paul Barker, the editor of *New Society* magazine. Such was the furore that, for a time, the leak and ensuing investigation into the breach of security led the national news. With Malcolm's permission I quickly owned up to being the author of the piece so that I could then help direct the political debate onto the issue of Child Benefit rather than the breach of the Official Secrets Act.

The leak of papers that the Prime Minister had personally reclassified as 'secret' led to an overkill reaction by government that, itself, ensured the subject matter of the leak received continuing coverage. From the moment – vividly described in this book – when I received Malcolm's notes, I never referred to the leaker as anything other than 'Deep Throat'; even in conversations with Malcolm himself. I gave as many TV interviews as possible so that I could talk about Child Benefit, but I also kept Malcolm up to date with who had interviewed me and what I had said. This was to minimise the possibility of him being trapped into an admission should he be interviewed by the celebrated Commander (Roy) Habershon of the Special Branch, who had been entrusted by the Prime Minister to spearhead an official enquiry.

A mega security leak was, however, not the only force making political weather. Tackling child poverty was a cause close to the Labour Party's heart. The leaked papers showed the Government acting less than honourably and the deceit practised on trade union leaders and backbench MPs alike inflamed opinion. Thanks to Malcolm's actions, the Government found itself on the run.

I have recalled elsewhere[1] the moves that were made to ensure that the Government recommitted itself to the introduction of the Child Benefit scheme in the following year. But all of this would have come to nought without Malcolm's courage in leaking these papers. He and I were as guilty as hell in breaking the Official Secrets Act. He certainly and I possibly could have gone to prison. As his autobiography indicates, he was placed under considerable stress.

Yet without Malcolm's actions there would have been no Government U-turn. It would never have been a possibility without his bravery. The terrible struggle he had with, on the one hand, his sense of decency and loyalty to public service, and, on the other, his commitment to a cause of combating child poverty, is powerfully recalled in this book. What Malcolm doesn't claim for himself, is that his name should be recorded in history books as 'Mr Child Benefit'. Yet that is how I believe we should regard him.

Illegal though it might have been in every technical sense, his conduct as a young, civil servant with principles was entirely in keeping with his sense of moral decency that is so apparent in his book. Knowing that most of it was written after he knew he was dying gives us certainty that his sense of values, so thoughtfully presented in his own words, remained strong with him to the end. He believed in no God, yet he was one of the most moral people I have known. He was principled, but his principles were not determined by calculation, and certainly not as a form of indulgence. They were a deliberate choice.

His political style was, likewise, not one that simply came from his temperament. It was made by choice. Politics was for Malcolm an ethical vocation. In that sense he was very traditional. So much of the early Labour Party was made up of ethical socialists and these, importantly, included his own father. Like Clement Attlee, they couldn't abide all the mumbo jumbo of Christianity, but adopted the best of Christian ethics. To this choice Malcolm brought a high intelligence that ensured that he was never simply tribal, although for the whole of his life his political loyalties were ever with the Labour Party.

Another attractive aspect of the personal values that Malcolm espoused and put into action as politician was his sense of stewardship. His role as servant or steward was not assumed by any false modesty and it was perhaps best seen in his relationship with his constituents. He wanted and loved the role of MP; not because it changed his status, or elevated him in any way, but because it allowed him better to serve people, especially the most vulnerable. He brought their voice to the floor of the House of Commons as no one else could. He became the Member of Parliament for Croydon North in 1992 and over the whole 20 years he missed only one constituents' surgery. After receiving his diagnosis of terminal cancer he was determined to act as a good constituency MP for as long as he could and his commitment to the people that sent him to represent them at Westminster continued to the end, although, by then, he was gravely ill.

Although it took needlessly long for his abilities as a politician and policy maker to be recognised, he became a Minister in 1999 and remained in government for the next nine years. Malcolm loved being a Minister simply because it allowed him to get things done. Making the best use of his talents was yet another admirable aspect of his character. There were few who could present the Government's case better, and even fewer whose beautiful sentences would be laced with humour – self-mocking on occasions, and invariably gentle with his opponents.

At our last meeting he talked about being the Minister for Lifelong Learning, which was possibly the role he loved most. It allowed him to open doors for those who had found them all too securely barred against them. He also recalled his time at the Department for Work and Pensions where, it would be fair to say, he knew as much about social policy as any Minister for the whole of the post-war period. Here, again, what mattered to Malcolm was not the knowing, but the doing. As Pensions Minister, for example, he took over a Private

Member's Bill to protect pension funds and was – as his autobiography shows – justifiably proud of it. His practical approach to the beneficial use of political power was no less apparent in his two terms as Minister for Energy and then as the Prime Minister's Special Representative on International Energy Issues: warning the country over the long term security of its energy supplies. He was active in drawing attention to the shortfall that we now face in our energy needs, and in trying to rectify this.

In each area of government where he served, Malcolm left a legacy. But it is necessary to remember that he was doing just that well before he became a Minister. The principled leak of the Cabinet papers on Child Benefit stands out in his own account because it has had such positive and lasting consequences for generations of families with children. Even so, readers will discover that the political achievement of which Malcolm was perhaps most proud was steering his 1995 Private Member's Bill giving official recognition to the needs of carers onto the statute book. His determination to draw public attention to a quiet legion of individuals, young and old, whose unpaid work was too often taken for granted was unflagging. His political and diplomatic skill, working across party boundaries to secure his legislation, was consummate.

Malcolm's commitment to the cause of carers was a product of the empathy that benefited his constituents and his colleagues: he found it easy to put himself in the place of others. He was gentle and considerate and natural courtesy was rooted in so much of what he did. Yet his habitual gentleness was matched by reserves of courage whose depths he may not always have appreciated himself. In his autobiography, for example, we read about the visit in the early 1990s, that Malcolm, and two Parliamentary colleagues, paid to Sarajevo when the Bosnian war was at its height. The stance that he and his colleagues took was, at that time, unfashionable in the Labour Party, while the Conservative Government advised against travel as it was so unsafe. He went ahead because he believed in the cause and the need to raise awareness of ethnic cleansing and the other horrors being perpetrated in Bosnia.

His physical courage was matched by a moral courage that ran like a golden thread through his life. When incurable cancer was diagnosed, he and Maggie, faced the inevitable with extraordinary dignity and resolution. His sense of humour remained intact. On being asked by the unsuspecting about his success in losing weight, he would reply that it was easy on the 'Marsden Diet'.

One other aspect of Malcolm that I admired tremendously is, thankfully, captured with clarity in this final book. He was a visionary. He never gave up thinking: not in a random manner but with a constant, practical focus on policy. He believed, as few others did, that ideas matter and shape our world. He asked himself how might we make our society more equal: not in some dreary ration book sense of the term, but by enabling the barriers of wealth, power and social class that divide society to dissolve, bringing people closer together.

To the end of his life, Malcolm was thinking about the big social issues and about the future; not least the future role of the Labour Party following its defeat in the 2010 general election. We are fortunate that the papers Malcolm published in his final year, and now this autobiographical volume, reveal him at his best in applying democratic socialist values in a 21st century context; setting out, in particular, his vision for the welfare state. It is a programme for the future that pays proper heed to the past. It is one of his many parting gifts.

Frank Field

*Notes*

[1] Field, F. (1982) *Poverty And Politics*. London: Heinemann

# PART 1

# My Life

# 1.

## *Early Years*

In a beautiful rural setting in Hertfordshire lies Brocket Hall. It was once the home of Sir Charles Nall-Cain who became Lord Brocket in 1933. Curiously it was my birthplace, although I was no member of the aristocracy. This was by no means a 'silver spoon in the mouth' birth. It was, however, an interesting coincidence, given my future interest in politics, because the circumstances of my being born at Brocket Hall on 1st July 1947 were wholly due to the politics of the 1930s and the approach of war.

The second Baron Brocket, a Conservative MP, became a member of the Anglo-German Fellowship and of several anti-Semitic organisations. At Brocket Hall he hosted meetings for supporters of Nazi Germany, and in April 1939 travelled to Germany to celebrate the 50th birthday of Adolf Hitler. He was not the only pro-Nazi aristocrat, and the atmosphere of those grand homes is well depicted in *The Remains of the Day*, the novel by Kazuo Ishiguro. During the war he was interned, alongside others, on the Isle of Man. Brocket Hall became a maternity home and remained so until 1949 allowing me to be born there. My mother was convinced that she gave birth in a room where the German Ambassador, future Foreign Minister and war criminal, Joachim von Ribbentrop, once stayed.

My parents, Arthur Ernest Stanley Wicks, and his wife, Daisy (née Hunt) were Londoners, from Islington and Southwark, both from working-class stock. My father's father had been killed in the First World War in 1917, in Flanders, just one of an estimated nine million who died in that barbaric conflagration on both sides. Life must have been hard for the family. The young widow, left to bring up two children of her own – my father and his older sister May – cleaned offices in the City of London. But in one respect they were fortunate. They were allocated a flat in the Samuel Lewis Buildings in Liverpool Road in Islington. These were the first properties completed by the housing trust[1] that was set up with an endowment on the death of Samuel Lewis – the most respected and philanthropic moneylender of his day – to provide housing for the poor.

Before my father left school at the age of 14, he earned a few shillings on a Saturday at the local market. He also often helped the milkman with his rounds. Milk would be poured from a churn into jugs and other receptacles left outside front doors. My father would calculate things carefully and craftily so that there would always be enough milk left at the end of a round for him to drink himself. These were hungry times. Another crucial component of his diet would be bread and dripping. Playing with his friends in the Samuel Lewis buildings he would often call up to his mum who would throw out the bread, soaked in dripping and wrapped in newspaper, from the window of their flat. As a child, I sometimes enjoyed this cheap and succulent snack myself. But it has largely disappeared now; the victim of healthy eating and more affluent times.

My grandfather's death in Flanders must have had a profound effect on his son, my father. Growing up in the 1930s he became a convinced pacifist and a socialist. He had an apprenticeship at Negretti and Zambra[2] and the active trade unionists there influenced the development of his own politics. But my father, as war beckoned, realised that the company produced goods that would aid the military effort and decided to leave.

Although conscientious objectors were treated more fairly in the Second World War than in the First, there was still a requirement to go before a tribunal. They had, in a sense, to prove their pacifism. My father's own testimony before the tribunal was aided by a written reference from the Reverend Donald Soper, whose meetings in

Islington during that period my father had attended and acted as a steward. Some pacifists refused to do anything that might, even at second or third-hand, aid the war effort. That was not my father's position and, for much of the war, his work involved re-housing families in Shoreditch who had been blitzed out of their homes. Once he ordered a bakery to be broken into so that hungry families could be fed. On another occasion, while inspecting a blitzed house to see if any people remained in it, he fell from one floor to the next and was lucky to escape relatively uninjured.

This experience of re-housing the homeless was to shape much of his public work in the future. A government official suggested to him that he should stand for the Shoreditch Metropolitan Borough Council. He contested his first election in 1949 and his career as a councillor progressed to the London County Council (LCC) and later the Greater London Council (GLC). He served as chairman of both the LCC and the GLC. I therefore grew up in a family where public service was intertwined with both family life as well as my father's business interests.

From difficult beginnings my father built a successful small business in Islington. At one stage he owned two hardware-come-general shops and a working man's café (the Oxford Restaurant) in Cross Street. He was also an agent for the Liverpool Victoria Friendly Society, pedalling around on his ancient bicycle to collect pennies and shillings from those anxious to have some insurance, not least for their funeral.

Looking back on my childhood, I can see that my father was the hardest working person I have ever met. He worked for hours and hours each day, including Saturday, when his main shop was always open. On Boxing Day he would open the shop in the morning, sometimes accompanied by me, because he knew that some of his elderly customers would need more paraffin to keep their fires burning and keep warm. Once, when the cook was ill, my mother stayed up half the night making apple pies. And the next morning my father cycled all the way from Muswell Hill to Islington so that postal workers, carpenters and the rest should not go hungry. He kept and worked in one of the shops into his late seventies.

He somehow pursued his business interests while also working as a councillor, school governor, Chairman of the Lee Valley Park authority and fulfilling many other public commitments. Yet he never failed, when we were children, to take us to Alexandra Palace on a Sunday morning, where we would play incessant games of football or cricket.

*Muswell Hill*

For the first few years of my life we lived above a shop at 2A The Exchange at the top of Muswell Hill ('The Exchange' so-named because of a bus depot there). An early memory, before going to sleep, was watching the shadows and lights flicker across our bedroom ceiling as buses and other vehicles came up and down the hill. Although not aware of it at the time, my elder brother, Keith, and I were partners to an alleged incidence of what we might nowadays call 'anti-social behaviour' when I was aged only five. According to the local paper, our landlord, Mr Jacobs, whose china and glass shop occupied the ground floor, sued my father for possession of the flat where we lived. At the court hearing, Mr Jacobs produced a daily diary. One entry read:

> *The children jumped down the stairs, played hide and seek in and out of the rooms, played ball, screeched, and on the whole were a positive nuisance.*

My parents' version of events was that the landlord unjustifiably wanted them evicted. Indeed, in cross-examination it was put to the landlord's wife, Mrs Jacobs, that she had performed: "every dirty and underhand trick you can think of to get Wicks out". I am glad to say that the court sided with us. But in any case, soon after, my parents were fortunate enough to buy a house off Fortis Green in Eastern Road: a well-built, brick, three-bedroom semi. There was a severe housing shortage and my mother happened to hear about the opportunity from the former owners' housekeeper, during a visit to the Lyons Tea Shop in Muswell Hill[3].

My main memory about my early childhood is one of security and comfort with a loving family that I took for granted. Keith and I, often accompanied by our friend Bill, seemed forever to be playing football and cricket, down at Cherry Tree Woods, in our smallish garden and, yes, in the road. The motorcar infestation was still in its infancy, so we played safely enough opposite a maternity home. This institution was, however, guarded by a formidable oak gate and presided over by a no-nonsense matron. Not infrequently, our ball would be kicked over the fence. So, being the youngest of us three, I was cajoled into trespassing into the maternity home in order to recover the ball, while, at the same time, avoiding matron. It was a scary experience.

Some characterise the 1950s as a boring decade. I never thought that (if I ever thought about it at all). For many, it was a period of hard work, family stability, increasing home ownership and rising affluence. So when Harold Macmillan declared in 1957 that "most of our people have never had it so good", he articulated a truth that helped him and his Conservative Party to victory in the 1959 General Election.

I would describe the weeks and months that passed as incident-free if that did not leave out my experience of being almost obliterated by a Tizer lorry! I must have been about nine and had ventured up the road from my home and crossed the (quite busy) Fortis Green Road. Why? To collect conkers from a large tree. No doubt excited by my find, I must have run back straight across the road. There was a terrible (but fortunate) screech of brakes and I saw the vehicle bearing down on me, followed by a second Tizer lorry. Crates of my favourite drink flew off the back of the open-backed vehicle. I think a kindly woman passer-by was trying to comfort me when I saw the lorry driver advancing in my direction. It later turned out that all he wanted was to get some details to explain what had happened to his manager. But I took off at speed down Eastern Road to find the safety of my mother and home. I cannot recall experiencing any post-traumatic stress following this incident. What is more, I kept drinking Tizer.

## 'Prep' School

It may surprise some people to learn that my socialist father sent my brother and I to a private preparatory school, Norfolk House, and, then, to a minor public boarding school. He explained this later by saying that it was before the era of comprehensive education. My 'prep' school experience started badly and then climbed remorselessly towards a mediocre level of academic endeavour and achievement. Day One was a catastrophe. Like many an infant before and after, I had no desire to go to school. Screeching and screaming, I had to be carried into the classroom by my first teacher, Mrs Saunders. For weeks I found it difficult to enunciate her name. Each day on the way to school my mother would encourage me: "Say 'Saunders', 'Saunders'!" and I would reply with some garbled and fearful version of this perfectly simple name.

Graduating to the next class, I found Miss Bromit was much more to my liking. But I was certainly the class dunce and recall some remedial reading sessions. There was one particularly embarrassing incident. I must have been having a bad day (a quiet sulk, I suspect) when Miss Bromit announced that: "The whole class will sing this song – including Malcolm". It could not have been worse, thanks to that complicated word 'including'. I wasn't totally stupid and knew that it either meant I should join in – or, as an assessment of my singing skills, the complete opposite! I suspect I half-mouthed the words, no doubt about as convincingly as John Redwood[4], when he was Welsh Secretary, unable to sing the National Anthem *Hen Wlad Fy Nhadau* at a rugby match in 1993.

Our headmaster, Mr (William) Howit, was a man of great personality, with a distinguished full beard. He commanded the attention of the boys, and, though he could be strict, was also popular. He often wore a vivid mustard-coloured waistcoat and was more likely to wear a bow tie than a conventional one. He regularly took snuff and would occasionally invite boys to take, as he put it, "a scrunch of wuff". Discipline at the school was generally strict, and this included overseeing the boys' behaviour in the immediate locality. If, for example, in crossing a road we failed to tip our cap at a motorist letting us pass, we were in trouble if a teacher noticed this. One day a serious incident occurred. Something had been stolen from a sweetshop and at the next morning's assembly the headmaster demanded that the culprit own up. No one did. It must have been near the end of term, because the headmaster decided that we would all stay at school for an extra day and sit in our classrooms in total silence until the errant boy came forward. So we sat there silently all day; and, of course, no one admitted their guilt.

At Norfolk House I was good at sport and became the captain of both the school cricket and football teams. I could also run fast. So, after one sports day, I came home with about ten pieces of silverware which my rather horrified mother immediately started to fret about keeping clean. I suspect this early sporting achievement was largely due to the small size of the school, because, when I progressed to my second school, it became clear to me that I was not necessarily the best sportsman in the country after all!

One of my earliest political memories came in what must have been the run-up to the 1955 general election, when I was justifying my support for Labour in the playground to friends whose families leaned in the other direction. I remember clearly saying that Labour supported the poor, while the Conservatives supported the rich. I also remember asking my father to sort out for me the different names that I was hearing about – 'Conservatives', 'Liberals', 'Tories', 'Socialists', 'Labour' and so on. During one election I also remember one of our teachers, the Latin master Mr Goode, telling his class with evident enthusiasm about "good old Lady Gammans". This turned out to be a reference to Lady Muriel Gammans who fought a by-election to succeed her late husband as Conservative MP for Hornsey in 1957.

It was often the custom on the final day of term for our headmaster, no doubt to while away the time, to ask boys what they wanted to do when they grew up. On one occasion most seemed to want to join the Armed Forces: "Navy, sir!", "Marines, sir!" and so on. When it came to my turn I said I wanted to be a politician. All the other boys roared with laughter; although I suspected most of them of not knowing what the word 'politician' meant.

My scholastic performance at Norfolk House, as previously indicated, was mediocre at best. However, there was some suggestion that I should apply for a place at Highgate School, a leading private school in North London for day pupils, so I duly took the so-called Highgate papers. Most of the tests were a complete mystery to me. I had never sat an IQ test before, nor been tutored in them, and it just struck me as so much mystifying gobbledegook. Naturally, I failed. My father had, however, heard about Elizabeth College, a boarding school on the island of Guernsey that had been recommended to him by a schools inspector he knew. My older brother went there and I followed three years later. I have had to explain many times in my life just how and why a boy from north London was sent to be educated in the Channel Islands!

# 2.

# *The Channel Islands*

My first trip to Guernsey started with a rendezvous of boarders and teachers at London's Waterloo station, followed by a train to Weymouth and then the ferry to St Peter Port. It was initially a strange experience for a 14-year-old Londoner and the first time I had been away from my parents. Although I never talked about it to anyone, I suffered appalling homesickness. In my diary I would number each day in a kind of countdown until the date when I would return home again. I clearly remember the despair of realising that there were, say, still 80 or 70 days left. I think now about the boys there who had been at boarding school since the age of six or seven. Some were being educated away from home because their parents lived abroad and others, perhaps, because they came from "broken homes". I do, now, wonder what they went through at those tender ages. Of course, my brother was already there at Elizabeth College and each week he and I would receive a letter from home. He was given it first to read and would then hand it on to me. Within a couple of weeks of my arrival, I remember passing my brother in the school quadrangle. He passed me the letter and, rushing to a lesson, told me: "Your rabbit's dead." I doubt that this did much to cheer my mood at being so far away from home.

The Elizabeth College boarding house consisted of only 80 or so pupils, because most of the school was made up of day boys. We sang from the public school hymn book and the school was a member of the Headmasters' Conference. A 'minor' public school would be an apt description, but it was one with a very long and colourful history, having been founded in 1563 on the orders of Queen Elizabeth I. As a boarder, in particular, my life was very regimented. An older boy, a prefect, would enter the dormitory every morning at about 7am loudly ringing a bell. We were then expected to run round the school quadrangle a few times to wake ourselves up, before showering and changing in readiness for the school day. Once, for a few weeks, the headmaster, who was also our housemaster, got it into his head that we would all be much more alert if we plunged into a cold bath – a very cold bath – before showering. Fortunately this experiment in what the Victorians might have called 'muscular Christianity' did not last long. Nor, happily, did it result in any early deaths.

*Faith, atheism and military conscription*

After the school assembled in the quadrangle each morning, we would all troop down the Grange to church at St James the Less. There would be a short service, including a hymn. At the boarders' evening assembly there would be another hymn. We also had to attend church service on a Sunday morning. We certainly had our full dose of enforced religious observation, but I can never be certain whether this was the reason why, during my time in Guernsey, I became a convinced atheist.

A few years earlier, despite being brought up in a non-religious household – my father was certainly an atheist – I had briefly dallied with Christianity. At one stage, probably when I was 10 or 11, I even thought through my own prayer. I worked on this quite hard, starting from the thought that to pray simply for oneself or one's immediate family was somehow selfish. There were doubtless all sorts of people in the world who needed help from God and I should reflect this in my own prayer. I also remember thinking that probably there were people elsewhere, somewhere out there in space, whom God should look after, too. So I ended up with this formulation, which became my own prayer, though for how long I do not know:

*Please God would you bless everyone and make them well if it pleases you – everybody, everyone and everywhere.*

I also remember clearly the last prayer I offered up at a time when my Christian beliefs were on the wane. It was the day the Labour leader, Hugh Gaitskell, died. I had met him a year or so earlier, when my parents took me to a Labour social, I think at Shoreditch Town Hall. I was shocked that such a young leader could be dead and that prompted me to address my last few words to a God that very soon I would not believe in.

I recall there were some rigorous discussions about religion in the school dormitory, not least due to the presence of my good friend, Nick Reade. Nick had decided that he wished to become an Anglican priest and so, with all the originality of schoolboys, we nicknamed him 'the Vicar'. Often on a Friday he and I would walk together to the local newsagent; he to collect his copy of *The Church Times*, me to pick up *Tribune*, the left-wing political weekly. Nick certainly did, in time, become a vicar. But I still can't help feeling that we rather under-estimated the future Bishop of Blackburn.

After my early homesickness, I grew to like life at the College, not least because of the challenges it presented. One such was the Combined Cadet Force, usually known as 'the corps'. This was, in practice, compulsory for all boys. It was only years later in public schools that those who objected to conscription could opt to do community service of some kind. It would be putting it mildly to say that I did not take to the Cadet Force. Following in my father's footsteps, I was a pacifist by inclination and for a time was even a member of the youth wing of the Peace Pledge Union. Therefore, the idea of putting on an army uniform, marching up and down and being taught how to use (admittedly out-dated) rifles did not appeal to me.

But with the benefit of hindsight I can see how it satisfied my rebellious instincts. While the keenest boys seemingly spent hours polishing their boots and putting a whitening compound called 'Blanco' onto their webbed belts, I would be deliberately dilatory about cleaning my kit. On the parade ground I marched in as relaxed a fashion as possible. One day, at the height of my conscientious objection, I refused to take part in a map-reading exam – no doubt on the grounds that this was, in its own way, preparation for mass slaughter. I simply signed my name in the allotted space. This led to a thorough dressing down by the teacher who was our commanding officer. Another time I had to go to a teacher, also a CCF officer, during mid-morning break because of some failure to abide by strict military routine. Our discussion went badly and I suspect that this bluff Yorkshire man was unimpressed by my somewhat sarcastic approach to militarism. He got so angry that he hit me (admittedly not very hard) in the chest. I rather regarded this as a victory for the non-violent protest movement.

What I enjoyed most was sport, of which there was an abundance at Elizabeth College. I saw myself as a good sportsman, but quickly found how much more difficult things were than at prep school. Aside from the increased competition, I suffered a blow at the start of one football season when, going in for a high ball, my left knee suddenly cracked and I was left in agony on the ground, swearing the few swear words I knew. I discovered later that my cartilage had gone. I should have had it sorted out surgically, but in those days this was not a straightforward operation. Instead, my knee was strapped up and I hobbled around for most of the remaining football season. To aid my rehabilitation, I was given a walking stick and must have developed a habit of twirling it around somewhat ostentatiously. Certainly one senior teacher, Mr Collenette, was heard to observe, "Wicks doesn't use his stick, he wears it!" The cartilage went again the next term when I was playing in goal in a hockey match. I had never played hockey before the age of 14 and decided that going in goal was the only way I could use my feet to good effect. Being a dangerous position, it also allowed me to dress up in some extravagant gear, and this, no doubt, appealed to my sense of style. My most momentous sporting achievement was winning the school's under-15s 100 yards race on Sports Day. I have often said since that this is my major lifetime achievement – and I have only been half joking.

If compulsory religion was intellectually stimulating and compulsory military training energising (albeit in ways not intended by the Sergeant Major) the scholarly part of my schooling – though no doubt important– was hardly satisfactory. I only succeeded in gaining five passes at GCE (General Certificate of Education) and they did not exactly cover a wide disciplinary canvass: English Language, English Literature, Scripture, British History and European History. Somehow I managed the extraordinary feat of failing British Constitution; something that afforded me periodic amusement during my Parliamentary and Ministerial career. Certainly no one at Elizabeth College ever suggested that I might go to university. In fact, I don't think that anyone during my entire schooldays ever suggested to me that I might do anything in particular in the future.

## Political stirrings

Looking back, I can see that my political and intellectual interests were growing, but in ways that bore little relation to my school studies – with the possible exception of history, which I greatly enjoyed. I formed a school group of the Campaign for Nuclear Disarmament (CND) and would send for badges, copies of the CND newspaper *Sanity* and the campaign songbook. One Easter, when aged about 15, a school friend and I decided to join the Aldermaston March[5] to London, camping out in schools and marquees along the way. Before setting off, we made a simple banner, using a white sheet, emblazoned with 'Guernsey YCND'. After about 40 minutes it grew too heavy to carry comfortably and we threw it in a ditch. However before this act of fly-tipping was carried out, a freelance photographer snapped the unlikely scene of two English schoolboys, who merely happened to be at boarding school in Guernsey, apparently demonstrating that the island's youth was fully behind unilateral nuclear disarmament. The photograph duly appeared on the front page of the *Guernsey Press*. This did not impress one of my friend`s mothers whose husband worked at the Scottish base for the submarines that carried Britain's Polaris nuclear missiles.

The four-day march from Aldermaston was an exhilarating experience. There were people from so many different backgrounds and shades of political opinion – pacifists, trade unionists, Quakers, teachers and other professionals. There was, of course, a strong contingent from the Labour Party, but also communists and other fringes of an eclectic and somewhat bewildering Labour movement. I saw the colours of the banners, heard the chants – *"Och, och, there's a monster in the loch. And we dinna want Polaris"* – and learned the songs. After that first year it was a regular occurrence for me to join the CND march. It was, I guess, my first real political commitment.

My support for CND, including occasional visits to their office in London, had one peculiar sequel that I only learned about three decades or so later. A school friend had joined the Army and made a successful career. He told me that on one occasion he was being interviewed for a special and, no doubt, sensitive posting or mission. He was subjected to tough interrogation. Had he ever been involved in any political or subversive organisation? "No," replied my friend who was almost certainly a Tory. "Let me put that question to you again" said the interrogator. "Any involvement in any political or subversive organisation?" Again my perplexed friend replied, "No". This went on for some time before the interrogator said: "But is it not the case that, together with Wicks, X,Y and Z, you were a member of school CND in Guernsey?" He protested that that was all a bit of a laugh for him and he only joined to get the badge. It is a curious story and no doubt we should all feel relieved that, at the height of the Cold War and so close to the Cuban missile crisis of 1962, our Secret Service was monitoring and keeping files on the activities of 15-year-old schoolboys in the Channel Islands.

The situation in South Africa and the struggle against apartheid was another early passion during my teenage years. Given that the only newspaper available to us at school was the *Daily Telegraph* (no doubt for the cricket results) and that we had no access to TV or even radio news, I'm not quite sure how I was able to follow the Rivonia trial and hear about the plight of Nelson Mandela and his colleagues[6]. It was an issue that gripped me, and at Elizabeth College we organised some kind of collection for Christian Aid, in support of the African struggle for equality. I placed a poster on the school notice board and from the row that followed you would have supposed that I had put up the most subversive kind of literature. (Though in a way, I suppose I had.) Later an apologist for the South African white nationalist regime was called in to present his arguments, while those of us opposed to the apartheid system were left to pen anonymous or pseudo-anonymous letters to the local newspaper. This proved very successful. In one letter I wrote:

*The time for letters of protest, vigils and petitions is fast running out. The only practical solution now is a World boycott on South Africa's goods, and who better to start it than Britain? We buy nearly one-third of South Africa's total export and the money they receive from these they put to good use, buying Saracen armoured cars, guns, Buccaneer aircraft, frigates and tear gas – all "made in Britain". So the time has come to boycott, which the President of the now outlawed African National Congress himself calls for.*

*If this is not tried and made to succeed, the answer to the problem may well become a bloody one. The Africans, realising the impossible situation, will revolt, and terror and death will replace tolerance and reason. I am personally against violence of any sort, but I live in a democratic and free country. If I was black, disenfranchised and trampled on by a white minority, I fear my pacifism would be more strongly tested.*

Letters to the *Guernsey Press*, either about apartheid or nuclear disarmament, were my first offerings to the literature of political discourse.

At about this time I bought my first serious, non-fiction book. Published in 1961, Bertrand Russell's *Has Man a Future?* cemented my concern about nuclear weapons. I became an admirer of Russell's work and during the coming months purchased a number of his other titles. I was enormously impressed by the range of his interests and his genius for both philosophy and mathematics. I dabbled with the former, but stayed clear of the latter. I never discussed any of these books with teachers and I expect that they would have been surprised to hear that I was reading them.

It was at about this time, too, that I first heard the music of Bob Dylan. It must have been his second album[7]. Up until then my love of pop music was centred around not only Elvis, but also, in particular, Buddy Holly whose untimely death made a huge impact on me when I was 11 years old. (The first single I ever bought was *It Doesn't Matter Anymore*.). It was also the era of Eddie Cochran, Cliff Richard, Gene Vincent, Roy Orbison and so many more. Then along came Dylan and also The Beatles and other groups that transformed the mid '60s.

It was Mr Dylan who undeniably made the biggest impact on me. His cries for freedom and human rights, the stories he told in his songs all have significance for me. For example, The *Ballad of Hollis Brown* who "lived on the outside of town"; *The Lonesome Death of Hattie Caroll*, a black maid who was gratuitously killed by a white tobacco farmer; the warning that, *A Hard Rain's A-Gonna Fall* and the more optimistic *Chimes of Freedom*. His powerful poetry and song provided an emotional content to complement what I was beginning to find out about the dangerous, cruel world in which I lived.

## On meeting Margaret

As must by now be apparent, I had a kind of love-hate relationship with Elizabeth College, although 'love' and 'hate' both seem rather too strong. I look back on my three years in Guernsey with fondness and, yes, some nostalgia. They did, after all, bring two undoubted benefits to my life. One of the great advantages of Elizabeth College, sitting towards the end of the Grange in St Peter Port, was that, at the higher end of the road, resided the Ladies' College. This was inhabited by pretty and, to my mind, confident girls who seemed far more mature than the boys at college; no doubt because they were so. Although fraternisation was hardly encouraged, it nevertheless took place. And so at the age of 16 – having first met briefly at 14 – Margaret Patricia Baron and I started 'going out' together. Known as 'Maggie' to her friends (not altogether to her liking) her home was on the neighbouring island of Alderney; so she lodged, while at school, with a family on Guernsey. And that was the start of our life together.

The other gain – entirely related – from my time at college was an introduction to the Channel Islands and, especially, Alderney. Maggie and I were married there in 1968 and frequently returned, often two or three times a year. It has always been to me an extraordinarily peaceful escape; a chance to blow away the cobwebs and relax.

But all that lay in the future when – halfway through my A-level course – my father decided it was time I left Elizabeth College and sought to improve my qualifications back in London.

## A-levels in London

I count myself lucky to have gone to the north-west London Polytechnic, there to do a one year A-level course. My subjects were economics, history and British constitution. During my initial interview, in a building above a supermarket in Camden High Street,

I was struck by the mature atmosphere and the way in which I was treated as an adult. My interviewer even called me Mr Wicks!

My fellow students were mostly older than me and many were from overseas, including two or three from Nigeria. I took my studies seriously and was encouraged, in particular, by my British constitution teacher, Mrs Rover. She was the first teacher ever to suggest that I might go to university. The problem was my far from impressive list of GCE 'O' levels. I received rejection after rejection from the universities I applied to. The sole exception was the London School of Economics (LSE).

3.

# Social Policy and Protest at the LSE

I remember my LSE interview very clearly. It was chaired by Professor David Donnison, accompanied by two other lecturers from the Department of Social Science and Administration. A new undergraduate degree in social policy was about to be launched and I had expressed an interest in this, rather than the sociology degree that I had applied for. Fortunately I was able to talk about housing policy and the reform of London government, both subjects that I knew a little about thanks to my father. I was offered a place, subject to my getting at least two 'B'-grades at A-level. No doubt encouraged by this, I worked even harder at the polytechnic. I was thrilled when the results came through – two 'B's and a 'D' – though my grades now seem modest in an age when so many students get three A*s (with compulsory hugging and kissing for the benefit of TV cameras).

From day one I loved being at the LSE. I felt lucky to be there. Like the polytechnic, it felt like a very adult, mature and challenging environment; but much more so. There were a large number of postgraduate students and also overseas students. The degree course I had enrolled for focused on social policy and administration – essentially the study of the welfare state – but took a very broad approach. We were examined in economics, statistics, government, sociology, social history and we also studied psychology and philosophy.

The department was headed by Professor Richard Titmuss, who was very much the founding father of social policy studies in Britain. He was a truly inspirational figure, through his writing, his teaching and his sheer presence. Alongside him were a talented group of teachers and researchers including my own tutor, Professor David Donnison. David, an expert on housing and member of an important committee on housing in Greater London (the Milner Holland Committee), subsequently advised the Labour Government of the day on rent policies. His colleague, Professor Brian Abel-Smith was a renowned expert in health services and social security. In 1965 his seminal work with Professor Peter Townsend, *The Poor and the Poorest*, highlighted the plight of families with children on very low incomes and led to the formation of the Child Poverty Action Group. As students we fully appreciated having teachers who were in the forefront of social reform, even if it meant some cancelled seminars when they were called upon to advise Ministers. My interest in social policy was already strong, mainly through my father's local government work. But now I had the opportunity to study the subject more thoroughly and academically. It became the subject that has largely dominated my career.

*Rhodesia and the 'Battle of the Strand'*

My first term at LSE in 1965 was memorable, however, for rather different reasons. In the then British colony of Southern Rhodesia, Ian Smith, the Prime Minister, had issued a unilateral declaration of independence in the name of his minority, white settler, government. Smith's 'UDI' flouted the intention of Harold Wilson's Labour Government that Rhodesia should progress to independence under majority, black African, rule. It was a tense time and UDI became an issue that captivated radical students at the LSE and dominated debates in the student union. A march from the LSE, down the Strand to nearby Rhodesia House, was organised. Disappointingly, however, it clashed with a lecture that I was meant to attend and, perhaps foolishly, I still assumed at this stage in my student career that I should attend all lectures. I failed to go on the march and when I went home that evening my father, who had marched against the British Union of

Fascists led by Oswald Moseley in the 1930s, was thoroughly unimpressed. The next day a second march was planned and I was determined not to miss out.

We duly set off, several hundred of us, in the direction of Rhodesia House. The police were prepared and waiting for us, engaging in all sorts of tricks to divert us from our target. The *Daily Mail* subsequently described it as the 'Battle of the Strand' and in exaggerated tones reported that "chanting students fought a running battle with policemen along the Strand in London yesterday". I found myself outside the Adelphi Theatre where building works were underway and scaffolding led to a narrow path between the buildings and the road. I suppose we would call what happened 'kettling' nowadays, because officers positioned themselves at one end of this narrow pathway to prevent us going further down the Strand. It was mayhem, potentially dangerous and some students could be heard screaming for help. I was shocked, as only an 18-year-old can be, by the police tactics, which I had never witnessed before. I thought that something should be done, so approached a police constable and asked him for directions to the nearest police station so that I could make a formal complaint. He ignored me, as did a second constable. I then approached a rather burly sergeant and put in the same request. His response was to grab me by the collar and put me into the back of a 'Black Maria' police van, where several other students already sat.

As a consequence, I arrived more speedily than intended at the police station in Bow Street, which was handily situated next door to the magistrates' court. The scene there was pretty chaotic; a dozen or so students had been arrested together with one unfortunate employee of Stanley Gibbons, the Strand-based shop for philatelists, who was venturing to Rhodesia House in the hope that new stamps might be issued by the illegal regime. One by one, police officers came in to claim the students they had arrested and make out a charge sheet. After forty minutes or so, just three of us were left, as it were, unclaimed. The police sergeant who had arrested me then appeared and, looking at the three of us, said to the desk sergeant: "I'll deal with this lot!" We were charged and put in the cells. (I shared my accommodation with a mature student whom, I learned, had become a conscientious objector while serving in the RAF.)

The police put it to us that if we pleaded guilty we would be in court the next day. We would probably be fined a couple of pounds, and that would be the end of it. But I was definitely 'not guilty' and started to prepare my defence, even though it would mean a delay of several weeks before I came to court. That evening at home, having plucked up the courage to relate my new criminal history, I found my mother was dismayed and not at all sure what my father would say when he came in. He, too, was somewhat shocked. I reminded him that he had been unimpressed by my failure to attend the first march. I also learned later how he would regale fellow Labour councillors at County Hall about my exploits. While not so important as the campaign against Moseley and the 'Blackshirts' it was clearly worth a few points.

I prepared myself for court with some thoroughness, believing that my wrongful arrest was a huge slur on British justice – and one that my eloquence would no doubt resolve. Other prosecutions dragged on all morning in the Bow Street Magistrates Court and I was uncertain when my own case would be called. But eventually it came up. The arresting sergeant made up a wonderful story about how three of us had been acting together, shouting slogans right outside Rhodesia House. He told the court how he had, supposedly, warned us that if we did not move on we would be arrested. As we, allegedly, did not move on, he had warned us a second time. It seems we refused to move on again; so he had warned us the third and final time before arresting us. This story was so far from the truth – I was arrested a good distance from Rhodesia House and had never met the other two students before – that I became confident the magistrate (whom I later heard was on duty for the first time) would instantly see the truth of the matter. The sergeant, however, was taking no chances and a second police officer, a motorcyclist, appeared as a witness to corroborate, word for word, his concocted version of events.

Despite my penetrating cross-examination (rather in the style of television's *Perry Mason,* I now realise) my only hope was to deploy my star (and only) witness. My friend and fellow student, Tony Hall, had witnessed my arrest and knew the truth. And so the cry went out: "Call Tony Hall!". A huge miscarriage of justice was about to be prevented, save for the fact that… no Tony Hall appeared. The call went out again, and again no witness rode to my rescue. Tony later told me that he thought the case would not come up until the afternoon. So, since he was engaged in the pursuit of one of our fellow students, Phoebe, and wanted to have lunch with her, this seemed to him to be a more pressing priority than balancing the scales of justice.

My case collapsed. Faced with two police officers telling the same story and one student telling the truth, the magistrate sided with the police. I was fined two pounds. However, I came out 'quids in' because the LSE students union paid my fine and so, too, did my father. The National Council for Civil Liberties sought a police investigation into the whole fracas and later I met an inspector who dealt with my protests most politely. I have dined out on the story several times, as you might expect, and have come to see the funny side of it. Tony and Phoebe, who were married in 1968, remain my best friends, and, of course, lived happily ever after.

But I also took on board the serious side of the story. Up to then my dealings with the police had been uneventful. But I had now learned a harsh lesson: that when push came to shove police officers in court were prepared to concoct stories and rubbish the truth. I realised that, if they would do this so an 18-year-old student could be fined two pounds for wilful obstruction, it would not be surprising in future if such wrongdoings occurred in far more difficult and important situations. It did not make me anti-police, but it certainly opened my innocent, young eyes.

Such tales make me sound like a student radical, but this was hardly the case. Compared with many students at LSE, my political views would have been regarded as fairly moderate. For example, I joined the Labour Society, rather than the much more popular, Socialist Society, which was full of Trotskyites and other members of the far left, including some extremely well-versed radicals. I was never tempted to leave the Labour Party and was deeply unimpressed by the worldly unreality of the extreme left. I was already a member of my local Labour Party in Hornsey and although it was a party on the left, the basic issues we discussed at our General Committee (GC) and branch meetings were about things like housing, health and education. This gave me a grounding in the real issues affecting people that seemed some distance from the theoretical and ideological questions discussed at the LSE students union and in the pages of the Trotskyite magazines.

My time at university coincided with a widescale political awakening among students and, in Britain, it was LSE students who led the way. These were undeniably exciting times. The three great international issues of the day were the Vietnam War, the apartheid regime in South Africa and white minority UDI in Rhodesia. Yet few would have predicted the furore that greeted a decision by LSE governors to appoint the Principal of the College of Rhodesia and Nyasaland to become the School's new director. I felt sorry for their appointment, Dr Walter Adams, who found himself caught up in this controversy. But I also did not feel that the LSE authorities had acquitted themselves well. The LSE Students' Union, which often sat for hours and hours at a time and was attended by hundreds, decided on a student occupation of the LSE buildings. This went on for weeks. As a Londoner, I commuted daily to the LSE from Muswell Hill. This did not prevent me from participating in the LSE sit-in, including one or two overnight stays. But my LSE friends would tease me about my regular trips home, not least to enjoy fried egg and bacon that my mother, without fail, prepared for me each morning.

The so-called students' revolt at the LSE came as a major shock to the university authorities and rapidly spread as a tactic to other universities, notably Essex. Although I was a participant, I was never a leading one. Indeed, I only spoke rarely in the students' union. Although exciting in its own way, this kind of student politics seemed far away from the politics of the people that I was learning more about. My activities increasingly came to focus on the Labour Party, and later the Fabian Society and the Child Poverty Action Group (CPAG).

# 4.

# *Starting Married and Working Life*

Having graduated from LSE with an upper second degree, the most important thing to happen was that Maggie and I got married. Aged just 21, we felt it was the right time. We never thought about cohabiting – and in retrospect we didn't really know the word existed. It might have been 1968, but outside of a rather small metropolitan circle, I tend to doubt whether the 'Swinging Sixties' really occurred before 1970!

Maggie and I were married in Alderney, but had a civil ceremony, which I think may have scandalised a few elderly islanders ("They say he's an atheist!") However, my new wife's church-going family were remarkably tolerant. The ceremony took place in the family home – this was long before the UK relaxed where civil services could be held – and a rather splendid reception was held at the appropriately named Grand Hotel. We then flew off for our honeymoon at Llanberis in North Wales. We stayed at a comfortable, small hotel, though for the sweet course, we both seemed to eat 'Arctic roll' every night. I doubt if we ever ordered wine. Later, our children could not believe that we honeymooned in North Wales; their choice, when the time came, fell on rather more exotic locations.

We spent an energetic time walking the beautiful North Welsh countryside, sometimes hitching lifts to get around. Our biggest adventure was almost falling off Mount Snowdon. We had walked up the main path, but decided to come back by a more rugged route, albeit one described in our guidebook as suitable for hill walkers. Soon we were in unfamiliar terrain, with steep drops on either side, should a foot be misplaced. Eventually the landscape changed and large amounts of scree appeared on one side, which was the side we thought would lead us back to Llanberis. We feared, however, that, should we scramble down, the scree would tumble after us and engulf us in an avalanche. Yet there was not much choice; the afternoon was drawing to a close and the Arctic roll beckoned. We risked it – and survived.

## *Teaching and researching in York*

I had secured a post as a Junior Fellow in Social Administration at the University of York. Our new life there could not have been more welcoming and comfortable. My salary was an adequate £850 per annum, while Maggie earned rather more as a Research Assistant in the University's Chemistry Department. We were allocated a flat in Alcuin College and altogether felt we had landed on our feet. We made life-long friends in Michael[8] and Molly Meacher[9] and Jonathan Bradshaw[10], who started with me in the Department of Social Administration.

My duties were light. I was entrusted with the occasional lecture – my first was on the reform of local government – together with some small tutorial groups and research projects. The Department was purely post-graduate, which meant the students I was teaching were either the same age as me or, often, quite a bit older. My key tutorial group consisted of two very nice, but also very confident, female Oxford graduates. I often doubted that I had much to teach them, but we all got along fine.

During my two years at York I got involved with the local Labour Party, with the Child Poverty Action Group (CPAG) and with adult education, not least through the Workers' Education Association (WEA). The York Labour Party, at least in parts, was somewhat moribund. As only two or three others attended my first meeting of the Walmgate Branch, rather against my better judgement, I was promptly elected Chairman. But while I played my role at ward and

General Management Committee (GMC) level, other commitments were more interesting. Eric Butterworth, a lecturer in community work in our department, got several of us involved in adult education. This was my first experience and I enjoyed it greatly.

However, not all the people of Yorkshire were eager to hear my lectures. I was asked to teach a series of sociology classes in Tadcaster, a town lying between York and Leeds, most famous for its breweries. I prepared eagerly and set out on a little bus from York to the town, which I had never been to before. I arrived early at the school and shuffled through my notes. Half an hour later, when the class was meant to commence, I had shuffled my notes relentlessly. No one appeared. A quarter of an hour later a man rode up on his bicycle and introduced himself as the local WEA organiser. He looked around the forlorn, empty classroom: "I told them sociology would never take off in Tadcaster," he said. I got back on the bus to York having learned that the struggle for adult education could sometimes be a testing one.

Several younger members of the department were members of the CPAG and the community workers among them suggested that we should hire a stall on a Saturday in York market. So, next to the man selling clothing and shoes and on the next stall up from a greengrocer, we laid out our leaflets publicising social security rights. We advised local people on these rights and did our best to represent them. Those helping on the stall included Michael Meacher, Richard Bryant, who specialised in community work, and many of our postgraduates. For me it was an important learning process. The York CPAG group thrived and the Group's new national director, Frank Field, would often come to York. Frank and I, together with my wife, Maggie, became firm friends during this period.

Another episode from our so-called community work in York stands out in the memory. In a situation that is still today played out across the country, gypsies had moved on to a site close to the city. We did our best to help, and a photograph of me appeared in the *Yorkshire Evening Press* carrying a banner proclaiming, somewhat incongruously, that "Mothers of York Support the Gypsies". Apart from the small technical matter of my not being a mother, I am afraid that it was almost certainly the case that the vast majority of mothers (and fathers) in York did not support the gypsies.

My research did not progress particularly well. I was registered for a doctorate and my planned thesis focussed on the 1965 Rent Act: a study of policy development. However, my supervisor, the formidable Head of Department, Kathleen Jones, was a great authority on mental health issues and unsympathetic to my chosen subject. I suspect I also lacked focus. I became, for example, very interested in the events leading up to the 1915 Rent Act including the Glasgow Rent Strikes and the 'Red' Clyde workers' movement. Our department also became riven by dispute, much of it based on personality. Michael Meacher, in effect, led the opposition and I guess I acted as a kind of PPS (Parliamentary Private Secretary) to him. The anti-Jones camp had the numbers, but we were routed. Michael moved away to the LSE and as my two-year Fellowship ended, I was fortunate to be offered work in London. I owe it to David Donnison, by now the Director of the Centre for Environmental Studies (CES), for rescuing me from York. Doubtless the non-appearance of my 1965 Rent Act Study is a great loss to British scholarship.

*Exposing hypothermia*

Compared to the rough and tough times that graduates experience today, I found myself in the happy position of being offered two jobs: one at the CES and the other as a part-time lecturer at Brunel University. Surprisingly, given the important part that the social aspects of energy policy would play in my working life, my discussion with David Donnison about a new research project got off to a slightly hesitant start. He told me about a study of hypothermia that was being discussed. I had never heard the word before and did not have a clue what hypothermia might be. No doubt it is best to own up in this kind of situation. But I played for time. I quickly learned that Dr Geoffrey Taylor, a Somerset GP, had been agitating about the dangers of cold winter conditions for elderly people and in particular, the danger that their body temperature might fall so low that they became hypothermic. I quickly understood why David Donnison thought this might be up my street.

My second job offer came from Maurice Kogan, until recently a high-flying civil servant at the Department for Education, who had served as secretary to the Plowden committee on primary education. He was now at Brunel University, establishing a new Department of Government Studies. He was looking for a young lecturer in housing policy who could also do some mainstream teaching on social policy. This would be mainly at postgraduate level. I applied and was appointed, albeit on an understanding that ways must be found for me to undertake both jobs. Fortunately David Donnison knew Maurice Kogan from Plowden days and it was soon agreed that I would work at CES on the hypothermia study four-fifths of my time, leaving one day a week teaching at Brunel. After the first year I shifted to more of a 'half and half' arrangement. I think that both CES and Brunel did well out of the arrangement, but more importantly so did I – not financially, but in terms of hard work, experience and an opportunity to practice my lecturing skills.

On the hypothermia project at CES we took a great deal of expert advice about physiology and survey techniques in geriatric medicine. The National Institute for Medical Research, a branch of the Medical Research Council, had a division of human physiology where Dr Ron Fox had developed methods for measuring human body temperature. We were also joined by Professor Norman Exton-Smith, a leading consultant in geriatric medicine at University College Hospital. Dr Michael Green of the Royal Free Hospital became another partner. The polling organisation Opinion Research Centre (ORC) was commissioned to undertake the crucial survey work.

Although my expertise, such as it was at the age of 23, centred on the social aspects of this socio-medical study, I also acted as the study co-ordinator. Working with expert leaders in their fields, this at time required diplomatic skills. It was, to adopt that awful cliché, a 'steep learning curve'. I also needed to master at least some of the medical and scientific literature so I would be able to talk for a couple of minutes, with surface authority at least, about thermo-regulatory systems, the function of the hypothalamus, and the different ways to measure deep body or core temperature.

Our aim was to undertake a national survey, across Great Britain, involving around 1,000 people aged 65 or over. They would be asked a wide range of socio-economic questions, focusing, among other things, on housing and heating systems and their levels of income. But the really complex and critical question was how, in the circumstances of mass survey, we should measure the body's core temperature (mouth temperature being essentially a measure of the body's surface temperature).

As I have found throughout my work, even the most dry, technical and serious matters can turn out to have their funny side. For obvious reasons, given that temperatures were to be measured in the home (albeit by specially trained nurses) taking anal temperatures was ruled out. As a concept, it conjured up the image of our nurses arriving on the doorstep with instructions to present interviewees with a thermometer and explain what they would like them to do with it. Fortunately for all concerned, Ron Fox had devised a method that involved measuring core temperatures from freshly passed urine. While, at first sight, this seemed almost as user-unfriendly, he had designed a gadget that enabled survey participants to 'go' when they wished, and for the nurses to collect bottles at a convenient time. Using his method we must have secured one of the largest-ever random collections of urine!

Our research, first published in a journal, then later in a series of scientific papers, made an impact. In 1978, after I had moved on from the CES, my own book *Old and Cold: hypothermia and social policy* was published[11]. It presented detailed findings from our study and went on to explore the implications for social policy as they touched on social security, personal social services and domestic heating.

Our main conclusions were that a small, but not insubstantial, proportion of elderly people suffered hypothermia during the winter, defined as a core body temperature at or below 35°C (95°F) and that many more – some 10 per cent – had body temperatures low enough to be considered 'at risk' of developing hypothermia. However, we also discovered that, far larger numbers were living in exceedingly cold homes. Indeed, the vast majority of elderly people at that time experienced temperatures that were below recommended levels. This was not through choice. Our survey showed that substantial proportions of elderly people felt cold in winter and would prefer warmer conditions. As for those most at risk, we found that the very aged who received supplementary pensions were more likely to have low body temperatures than other, younger pensioners. We concluded this was probably due to poor health, declining physiological state and adverse social conditions.

Our findings were startling. Yet our survey was undertaken during a relatively mild winter at a time of relatively warm winters. Some 36 years later, I re-read the final paragraph of my book as something of a *cri de coeur*, illustrating just how much this study had affected me:

> *Sooner or later a very severe winter will occur again. How will our old people fare when this happens? Will the widespread anxiety that exists about hypothermia, the interest of the mass media, the campaigns of pressure groups and the concern of government be translated into positive action to ensure that Britain becomes a society where it is no longer possible to be both old and cold?*

I could not know then, but three decades later, when I was Minister of State for Pensions and then Energy Minister I found these were still-pertinent questions. But by then we were in an era of high energy costs and the tough questions were being directed at me.

# 5.

# *The Birth of Child Benefit*

As the clock reached midnight at the start of June 17th 1976 I was to be found intently listening to the BBC News on Radio 4. The lead item concerned a report being published in that day's edition of *New Society* magazine based on an unprecedented leak of Cabinet minutes. These detailed an unexpected U-turn by the Labour Government on its radical plans to introduce a Child Benefit. The leaked papers, it transpired, had been passed to the Director of the Child Poverty Action Group, Frank Field. He had, in turn, communicated their contents to the magazine.

To account for my exceptional interest in this breaking news, I should explain that two years earlier, I had departed academe to work as a civil servant. I had become a 'Social Policy Analyst' in the Urban Deprivation Unit at the Home Office. My new role was an imprecise one. The prime task was to help the team responsible for developing comprehensive community programmes, but I also had access to a wider range of government documentation concerning social policy. Papers about health, employment, education, crime, housing, social security and the rest, all came across my desk for comment. As a sometime student of social policy I was in my element. After several years as an academic studying and teaching these subjects, relying on inevitably dated texts and publications, I was seeing and influencing current policy papers.

Yet I always expected that my career in the civil service would be a brief one. This was not simply because I was on a relatively short contract. More importantly, unlike mainstream civil servants who have to put partisanship aside, I knew I could never serve a Conservative government. My loyalty was to Labour, no matter how frustrating that could often be during those difficult years in the 1970s. It is also relevant to mention that I had maintained my near-founder membership of the Child Poverty Action Group and, while lecturing at Brunel University, produced CPAG branch newsletters and also contributed to the Group's national journal *Poverty*. I stayed a member when I joined the Home Office, although I could not play an active role.

I was, in other words, committed to the cause. I regarded the abolition of child poverty as a priority. I considered that the existing system, with an inequitable division between family allowances and child tax allowances, was in need of reform. I, therefore, fully supported the Labour Government's policy proposals for a new Child Benefit merging family allowances and child tax allowances into a single, non-means tested benefit.

The Child Benefit system that we know today owes its origins to a long campaign to gain recognition for the principle that children impose costs on families that cannot be met through the wages system alone. The concept of family allowances as a regular and universal system did not gain acceptance until the early 1940s. While the case for family allowances, or 'family endowment', appealed to a broad political spectrum, the main argument advanced was the need to support poor families. For example, the Family Endowment Society formed by Eleanor Rathbone in 1917 argued for direct state subvention to all families (in and out of work) with dependent children, at a rate sufficient to provide for each child at subsistence levels.

> *Children are not simply a private luxury" she wrote. "They are an asset to the community, and the community can no longer afford to leave the provision of their welfare solely to the accident of individual income.*[12]

In 1943, the wartime coalition government committed itself to the introduction of a universal, tax financed family allowance system, implementing proposals included in the 1942 Beveridge Report on social insurance. The Family Allowance Act was passed in 1945.

To understand the eventual controversy over Child Benefit it is important to note how family allowances in the post-war period developed alongside a different system of child tax allowances. These were designed to increase the net pay of the wage earner, normally the father. By contrast, the family allowance was usually paid to mothers. The complexities and inconsistencies inherent in these two systems came under critical scrutiny from both the Conservative government of 1970 to 1974 and the opposition Labour Party. Edward Heath's administration published a Green Paper in 1972 outlining radical proposals for a tax credit system. This envisaged the integration of much of the taxation and benefits systems. Child credits would have been introduced replacing both family allowances and child tax allowances. The scheme was never introduced having being overtaken by the election of February 1974, which saw the return of a Labour government under Harold Wilson. However, the proposals relating to families with children survived in a new guise.

Under the Child Benefit Act passed in 1975, family allowances and child tax allowances were to be replaced by a unified Child Benefit: paid to mothers as a tax-free, flat-rate sum in respect of every dependent child up to 16 (or 19 if in full-time education). The passing of the Bill coincided with International Women's Year and much was made of the intended transfer of child support payments from 'wallet to purse'[13]. The then Social Services Secretary, Barbara Castle, commented that a mother "certainly needs control of her own budget if the family is to be fed and clothed"[14].

So far, so good. The legislation was passed, putting into effect –at least in principle – a commitment made in Labour's manifesto for the second 1974 General Election that took place in November. But then the scheme started to run into serious political difficulties. The context, which needs to be understood, was that the British economy was not strong. Labour's Chancellors of the Exchequer, James Callaghan succeeded by Denis Healey, were anxious about public expenditure. This was also the era of incomes policy and the compact between the Government and the TUC that was known as the 'Social Contract'.

There was also some opposition within the higher ranks of the party to the very idea of universal provision. Frank Field recalls a conversation with Margaret Herbison, who had been Social Security Minister in the early years of the Wilson government. She recalled a Cabinet discussion in 1967 when the then Chancellor, James Callaghan, had argued for the introduction of a means-tested income support scheme for families[15]. So when the Child Benefit Act reached the statute book in 1975 attempts by backbench MPs to write in a date for starting the scheme into the legislation had been over-ruled by the Government. There had been hopes that the scheme would begin operation the following year, but financial pressures prevented this. Yet the Government had let it be understood that the full scheme would come into operation a year later.

By the spring of 1976, however, moves were afoot at the very top of the Government to scuttle Child Benefit. Indications of a possible U-turn had begun to appear in one or two newspapers. But it was the leak of Cabinet minutes to *New Society* magazine that exposed the full extent of the manoeuvring to trash the scheme. One key issue was the rate at which full Child Benefit would be paid from April 1977. Barbara Castle, whose dedication to Child Benefit could not be doubted, had been sacked from the Government by James Callaghan when he succeeded Harold Wilson as Prime Minister in April. The reshuffled cabinet received a memorandum from David Ennals, the new Social Services Secretary. This made it clear that families with children were getting substantially less state support than the Tories had provided in 1970, 1971 and 1972, and also less than under Labour in the late 1960s. The memorandum to the Cabinet concluded:

*If we continue to let child support to be eroded by inflation, the whole scheme will be condemned as a trick to give children less, not more.*[16]

Ennals argued for an initial Child Benefit rate of £2.90. Denis Healey, the Chancellor, countered, in a note of his own, that the Treasury was thinking in terms of £2.50 a week, plus 50p premium payments for the children of single-parent families and larger families.

The argument moved on to a point where the Cabinet minutes of 29th April 1976 show that members began to discuss the effect that a withdrawal of child tax allowances would have on negotiations for the next stage of incomes policy. The Cabinet concluded that it might be better to postpone the Child Benefit if the funds were not available to introduce it at an acceptable rate. As Frank Field subsequently wrote in *New Society,* based on the leaked Cabinet minutes:

*After the 4 May cabinet meeting, the new Prime Minister began working behind the scenes. At the cabinet meeting of 6 May, he reported receiving an "excellent report" from the Whips Office which had created fresh doubts in his own mind about the political implications of introducing child benefit. The new Chief Whip, Michael Cocks, reported to the cabinet that, after surveying opinion (though the minutes do not recall whose opinion was canvassed), the introduction in April 1977 of child benefit would have grave political consequences which had not been foreseen when the bill went through the House of Commons.*

*In the ensuing discussions cabinet ministers expressed the belief that the distribution effects of child benefit could not be "sold" to the public before this scheme was brought in in April 1977. In summing up, the Prime Minister commented that to defer the scheme would also require careful public presentation. The two cabinet meetings of 4 and 6 May had scuttled the child benefit policy.*[17]

The role of the trade unions in all of this provides a crucial, and sometimes confusing, part of the narrative. As mentioned earlier some of the cabinet discussions were being leaked to two national newspapers. It was as a result of these leaks that trade union leaders who were committed to Child Benefit insisted on inserting a crucial phrase into the statement agreed by the TUC/Labour Party Liaison Committee at their meeting on 24 May. The statement insisted it was "of the utmost importance that the new Child Benefit scheme, to be introduced next year, provides benefit generous enough to represent a determined and concerted attack on the problem (of poverty)."

What the full trades union delegation at the Liaison Committee meeting did not know was that a smaller group of leaders – those who led the trade union side on the National Economic Development Council – had arranged to see the Chancellor of the Exchequer and other senior ministers later the same day. At the Cabinet meeting the next day (25th May) the Prime Minister asked the Chancellor to report on this meeting where the TUC had been asked to agree to a postponement of the Child Benefit scheme for three years. This had been argued on the grounds that losing child tax allowances would have an adverse effect on take-home pay. According to the leaked Cabinet minutes:

> *On being informed of the reduction of take-home pay, which the child benefit scheme would involve, the TUC representatives had reacted immediately and violently against its implementation, irrespective of the level of benefits which would accompany the reduction in take-home pay.[18]*

The Cabinet thereupon agreed that David Ennals should announce the effective postponement of Child Benefit that afternoon in the House of Commons.

As might be expected, the publication of normally secret Cabinet minutes in *New Society* three weeks later unleashed a storm of media and political interest. This centred on both the future of Child Benefit and on the use and abuse of official secrets (including the case for more freedom of information). In a Commons statement, Prime Minister Callaghan announced that a top-level civil service enquiry had begun into the leaks. And, as *The Guardian* reported on June 18th:

> *Mr Callaghan's announcement brought about an instant closing of the ranks within the political Establishment at Westminster.*

The Leader of the Opposition, Margaret Thatcher endorsed the view that the leak was of the utmost gravity. She suggested full police inquiries and perhaps even a tribunal of inquiry under a judge. When the leak inquiry, under Sir Douglas Allen, Head of the Home Civil Service, began its work, it soon became apparent that several score of Ministers and their officials would have to be interviewed. There was widespread speculation as to who was responsible for the leak, not least because several political advisers to the Government were closely associated with the Child Poverty Action Group.

The Government's decision to postpone the Child Benefit scheme and the shameful manoeuvrings revealed through the leaked Cabinet minutes, meanwhile, led to a storm of protest. Over 100 Labour MPs signed a Commons motion calling for implementation of the scheme. So much for the Chief Whip's backbench alleged soundings! Barbara Castle, who had become a member of the powerful government/TUC liaison committee, marched into battle with others to save Child Benefit.

Frank Field was at the centre of the storm (his informant was lying low). But it is hard to imagine anyone being better equipped to be at the centre of this kind of policy storm than the 33-year old, then, Director of the CPAG. When Frank was interviewed by Sir Douglas Allen, he was accompanied his solicitor, the distinguished lawyer Geoffrey Bindman, who was making his name as a radical specialist in the law of human rights. On this and more public occasions when he talked about the affair, Frank gave everyone the impression that he inhabited a colourful and mysterious world. Apparently it was not uncommon for brown shopping bags of government material (such as draft benefit regulations) to be left outside the CPAG's offices in Covent Garden. Frank also had a lot to say about his communications during this period with an informant he dubbed 'Deep Throat' – somewhat fancifully named after the government insider who helped *Washington Post* journalists Bernstein and Woodward to expose the Watergate scandal in America.

Cabinet members were among those interviewed by Sir Douglas Allen and his team. According to Frank's published account of what happened:

> *Cabinet ministers were interviewed if it was known that they were committed to the child benefit scheme (a pledge in Labour's 1974 manifestoes), or they believed in more open government (another pledge in both election manifestoes) or if they were deemed to be politically motivated (an attribute one might expect in all professional politicians at cabinet rank…). Cabinet members were to be interviewed if they qualified on one or more of these grounds, yet only a third of the Cabinet were questioned.*[19]

There was a story at the time that one Cabinet Minister, widely believed to be Tony Benn, was successful in resisting interrogation by Commander Roy Habershon of Scotland Yard, whose investigations followed up on Sir Douglas Allen's inquiry. He apparently informed the Prime Minister that if he was required to meet the Head of Special Branch, he would request the former Conservative Minister and future Lord Chancellor, Lord Hailsham, to be present with him at the meeting. Commander Habershon never bothered the Secretary of State again.

For my part, although I had not asked to see the official papers detailing the changes of policy on Child Benefit implementation, they came to me anyway in my room at Horseferry House in my policy analyst role. I paid them close attention. As days passed and I saw more documentation, including Cabinet papers, it was not so much the attempt to abandon Child Benefit that incensed me, but more the way it was being done: the manoeuvring, the downright lies, and the attempt to play off Labour MPs against trade union bigwigs.

The Prime Minister's "excellent report" from the Chief Whip was, frankly, a fabrication. The fact that, later, over 100 Labour MPs signed a Commons motion in support of Child Benefit testified to the enormity of the lie. Then there was the Government's efforts, at Prime Ministerial and Chancellor of the Exchequer level, to persuade the Cabinet that trade unionists, despite having known about the policy for a very long time, had suddenly turned violently against it. The fact that there was so much ignorance about Child Benefit at the highest levels – both in Cabinet and among some trades union leaders – also riled me. Had it been a straightforward matter of the introduction of Child Benefit being abandoned after an honest and open discussion in Cabinet, I would certainly have been disappointed. But I do not think that, as a 29-year old civil servant, I would have claimed the right to take further action. In the circumstances, however, I took what I regarded as an ethical decision. My view was that if a Labour Government was to abandon its policy, having connived and misled, then I had a duty to leak what happened to the papers – knowing full well that this would have repercussions – so that people would see the truth.

As I had signed the Official Secrets Act, I knew how important my decision was. I made extensive notes of the official papers, including the Cabinet papers. These were notes in my own handwriting (which has always been rather poor). I certainly went nowhere near a photocopier. I then met Frank Field and passed over my notes, outlining then, or maybe beforehand, what they were about. I should, perhaps, make it clear that neither Frank nor anyone else had put any pressure on me to leak the documents. It was solely my own idea.

There followed a meeting between me, Frank and Paul Barker, the editor of *New Society* (a wonderful magazine of the era). At the magazine's offices in King's Reach Tower, the editor cross-examined me carefully. He had no idea who I was and I guess he wanted to know where I was coming from on this – and whether the documentation itself was accurate.

Looking back, one remarkable aspect of the affair is that my wife, Maggie, and I stayed in close touch with Frank, as had been the pattern before the leak. Indeed, Maggie has a clear memory of Frank coming round for Sunday lunch a few days after *New Society* published its scoop. She remembers that he and I engaged in some serious discussion at the end of the garden. We also kept talking on the telephone and Frank would occasionally ask me what I thought 'Deep Throat' might be thinking. I suspect that I was not terribly forthcoming.

At a personal level, the furore that followed the leaking of the Cabinet documents was a most difficult time. When I caught my train up to Victoria station on the day of publication, I would not have been surprised if police officers were waiting for me. I opened my office door in Horseferry House with some trepidation. Various people in the Urban Deprivation Unit were discussing the leak and I recall one colleague even saying to my face that he wondered if it was me. I lost some weight during this period, but it is not a diet I would recommend. The enquiry process went on for a very long time and when the official Whitehall investigation closed – with Sir Douglas Allen reporting to the Prime Minister that the informant had not been found – it was not the end of the affair because a follow-up investigation by Special Branch was launched under Commander Habershon. There was a suggestion that the Commander always got his man.

I am conscious that it must also have been a very difficult time for Ministers, officials and special advisers who came under the spotlight, including several I knew well. I was resolved, of course, that should anyone be falsely accused, or in any way suffer, I would come forward and own up to what I had done. At the time, and even three and a half decades later, it seems amazing to me that I was never interviewed or interrogated. Indeed, no one ever asked me officially about the incident. The official Whitehall enquiry noted that Home Office

Ministers, and therefore their private offices, received several copies of the papers. Yet the investigators' focus was clearly elsewhere.

So did the leak of Cabinet minutes save Child Benefit? Certainly, the Callaghan Government was obliged by the furore to backtrack and phase in the new payments over three years. Otherwise, as Frank Field has written, it is "more than probable that the Child Benefit scheme would have been postponed indefinitely". The economic and financial climate at the time scarcely lent confidence that the scheme would have been resurrected. Moreover, with Mrs Thatcher, the 'Iron Lady', leading the Conservative Party with all her insistence on public spending constraints, it is improbable that the administration she formed in 1979 would have prioritised universal support for families had it not already been in place.

Was I right to leak the cabinet papers? I still think I was. In the normal course of events civil servants, Ministers and special advisers should not leak confidential material. It goes without saying that matters relating to national security have to be heavily safeguarded. But regarding the introduction of Child Benefit there was, I felt, a moral issue. It simply could not be right that Ministers, at the most senior level, should manipulate internal discussions in such a way that the Cabinet itself was misled. I thought – and still think – that in those circumstances it was justifiable to leak or, putting it more positively, to let the wider public know what was going on.

I should also say that, following the *New Society* article, there was renewed interest in the over-draconian powers of the Official Secrets Act and a campaign for more open government was revived. Things of course are very different now. Leaks of all kinds regularly appear and many Ministers, officials and special advisers, in particular, leak to journalists as if it is part of their job description. When I became a Minister and, indeed, as a Shadow Minister, I never leaked anything to anyone. Maybe, at a personal level, that was because of my 1976 experience; but more importantly it was because I respected the rules of confidentiality surrounding government business.

6.

# Studying the Family

From the Home Office, I moved to the Civil Service College, based at Ascot, as a lecturer in social policy. But I was not keen to stay there for too long and, after a while, I saw an opportunity to move on. An advert appeared for a Research Director and Secretary for a new 'Study Commission on the Family'. It stated that the appointment would be part-time, but I wrote to the Chairman of the Commission, Sir Campbell Adamson, and sought to make the case for a full-time appointment. At first, I was not called for interview, but then Sir Campbell changed his mind. Although the favourites for the job were two eminent family researchers, he clearly felt that a wider number of interviewees might be helpful. I remember it being a hot sticky day as I arrived for the interview, and I also recall that it was probably the worst interview I ever gave. Indeed, one distinguished member of the Commission, Baroness Barbara Wootton, asked me at one stage if I had a degree. Apparently I had omitted this important information from my CV. But somehow I got through and I was offered the job on a full-time basis.

It was the start of a number of happy years working first for the Study Commission between 1978 and 1983 and then as Director of its successor body, the Family Policy Studies Centre (FPSC). The Commission's board was an august one, including Sir Campbell himself, who became a firm friend. He was a former Director General of the CBI and had become Chairman of the Abbey National building society. Frank Field – who became the Labour MP for Birkenhead in 1979 – was a board member, as was the distinguished sociologist Professor A H 'Chelly' Halsey. Peter Mandelson, the Cabinet Minister-to-be represented the British Youth Council, while a degree of political balance was achieved through the presence of Sara Morrison, a former Vice-Chairman of the Conservative Party. Sara had held her party post during the Heath years and it was said that when Mrs Thatcher took charge there was a race between Sara's secretary and the new leader's office to enable Sara to resign before she was sacked. There was also, of course, the formidable Barbara Wootton herself. She was one of the most eminent women in Britain, the author of twelve books and holder of twelve honorary degrees. She was also one of the first two women to be appointed life peers when Harold Wilson was Prime Minister. Then in her eighties, she possessed an intellect that shone through.

As the Study Commission was a brand new body, I started with no office and no staff and worked from home for the first few weeks. However, we had a generous grant from the Leverhulme Trust and soon Sir Campbell ensured that Abbey National supplied us with offices at 231 Baker Street. This address was deceptively similar to that of a distinguished fictional detective and gaping tourists would often be found outside our office. I once mischievously pretended to be Dr Watson's grandson, following an American enquiry, before hurrying on to my next meeting.

## Charting family change

I decided that the best approach for the Study Commission would be to publish useful papers as we went along, rather than aiming towards the more typical grand, final report. This is not the place to detail the research we undertook during those years, which is well documented. Our work was undertaken during an era of enormous change affecting the British family that threw up a myriad of issues. These can, perhaps, be summarised under three broad headings:

First, there was what might be described as the growing diversity in family patterns. It was always a rough exaggeration to say that the traditional family consisted of a husband and wife and children (thus forgetting how early mortality had formerly led to so much widowhood, not least following the First World War). Nevertheless, the post-Second World War period produced a social revolution. It experienced an increasing number of divorces, following the Divorce Law Reform Act of 1969, and a dramatic increase in the number of one-parent families. This latter development was a consequence not only of divorce, but also a growing tendency for children to be born outside of wedlock (in some cases with fathers who displayed no long-term commitment) and the break-up of casual relationships. Cohabitation was becoming more popular among different social classes and phraseology about 'living in sin' became increasingly historic. These were by no means victimless trends and children, as ever, were often the losers. One consequence was that, alongside economic circumstances, social factors were now contributing significantly to the extent of child poverty. These things were challenging to the traditional underpinnings of the welfare state. Thus, attempts by the state to understand family change and grapple with its practical consequences became – amid controversy over values and beliefs – an increasingly important issue in contemporary social history.

A second major trend was the interaction between work and the family and, principally, the growth of women's employment. Again, this challenged traditional policy assumptions. While William Beveridge was undoubtedly a progressive social reformer, many today would now register with some shock and awe the assumptions he made about family life in his 1942 report on *Social Insurance*, arguing that:

> *All women by marriage acquire a new economic and social status, with risks and rights different from the unmarried. On marriage a woman gains a legal right to maintenance by her husband as a first line of defence against risks which fall directly on the solitary woman; she undertakes at the same time to perform vital but unpaid service...*[20]

As documented by the Study Commission and its successor FPSC, many women into the 1990s continued to perform "vital unpaid services" in the home, while many husbands remained reluctant to do their share of the childcare, cleaning and cooking[21].Yet we also charted a steep rise in women's employment, including mothers with very young children. This was a development made possible, in part, by an increase in part-time job opportunities. Thus the phenomenon of the dual-earner family grew in significance with substantial consequences for public policy, not least the availability and costs of substitute childcare while both parents were working.

A third major trend involved looking not just at the nuclear family, but the wider, extended family. Indeed, the implications of an ageing population for family life and social policy became one of the major questions guiding our research. We investigated how it was often the family itself – usually, though not exclusively, its female members – who took on the main role of caring for frail, elderly parents and others in the family who needed significant support. Our work on family care and the role of the 'carer' was to influence strongly my later Parliamentary work and, in particular, the 1995 Carers Act that I introduced as a Private Member's Bill (see Chapter 9).

I enjoyed greatly my work at both the Study Commission on the Family and the FPSC, not just because of the richness and complexity of the subjects we were exploring, but also because it was the closest I had become to running a small business. The organisation was both a registered charity and a limited company, with me as company secretary. Of course, we did not survive through selling products as such, and most of our income came from either government or foundation grants. But these were not easy to obtain and we often led a fairly hand-to-mouth existence financially. We did, in fact, also sell products: namely, the many reports and papers that we published. I always enjoyed promoting these and I got a particular kick out of the production process.

We would start with an idea and seek the money necessary to activate it. Assuming success, there would follow months of research and writing until we were ready to go into production. In the early years of our work, when personal computers were rare in any office, the manuscript would have to be typeset and checked and corrected on printed proofs. However, we were one of the first research and policy groups to purchase a word processor – in those days a giant block of technology so full of complexity that only one staff member fully understood its workings. Subsequently, of course, all our staff were allocated PCs, although some objected to the expectation that – as academics and researchers – they would now have to type their own work. It was an exciting day when a new report arrived from the printers and I always enjoyed helping to carry the boxes up our office stairs, knowing we were near the end of the production line. But not right at the end, because we took publicity tremendously seriously, producing hopefully eye-catching press releases and holding numerous telephone conversations with journalists. Some reports, particularly if they coincided with a heavy news day, hit the dust. But our success rate was high, and it was not unknown for our reports to be carried on the front pages of national newspapers – and for the vast majority of newspapers, together with TV and radio, to cover and comment on them in some way.

At most, our staff never numbered more than eight or ten, but this gave me an experience of staff management. This was not always easy, dealing as I was with independent-minded researchers who perfectly properly had their own ideas about their work. Yet my responsibility was to try to mould this into some kind of overall identity and mission for the FPSC. I had to ensure that deadlines were kept and the flow of publications maintained. We were not the richest research body in London (far from it) but my aim was always to punch above our weight. I remember in the early days having a somewhat difficult meeting with one of our talented researchers. We did not see eye to eye on a particular project and she left the room without us reaching a conclusion. She went back to her office upstairs and then I heard an almighty crash. I heard later that she had thrown a chair against the wall.

# 7.

# *Parliamentary Ambitions*

From about the age of 12, I wanted to become a Member of Parliament. Many might consider this rather sad at so young an age, but it was certainly remarkable given that I had only the barest idea of what MPs did. By today's standards, it took me a while to fulfil my youthful ambition: I did not enter Parliament until I was aged 44 in 1992. But by then I had been a researcher, a university lecturer, a civil servant and Director of the Family Policy Studies Centre, and had, consequently, picked up a fair amount of experience along the way.

Despite my long-held intention, I didn't try very hard to find a seat before the final push in Croydon North West. I was enjoying my career and I also had a young family. I did, however, make one attempt to become the Labour candidate for Derby South. I must have ventured up to the constituency on about three occasions and received some early encouragement. Yet I failed to receive any Branch nominations and, when even the local Fabian Society failed to nominate me, I knew the game was up. One Margaret Beckett[22] duly became candidate and, at the 1983 General Election, the elected MP. I learned much from my failed Derby sojourn, and mainly that I felt a real phoney. At first I had no idea where Derby was and had to consult a map. Then, despite avid reading of the local newspapers for several weeks, I still had little knowledge about the place. In this I suppose I was no different from a succession of Labour politicians seeking a winnable seat, from Gaitskell to Blair. But it still felt unreal.

*Campaigning in Croydon*

Largely unwritten chapters of British political history are populated by the ghosts of would-be politicians who didn't make it into Parliament. Often this has been regardless of their talent, intellect and experience – their places taken, sometimes, by the single-minded and scheming, plus those content to persevere, travelling to a score or more of constituencies in search of success. A crucial ingredient is simply luck (or the lack of it). When Maggie and I first moved to Croydon in 1975 it was very much 'Tory Town' writ large: all four MPs were Conservatives and the Council had been in Conservative hands seemingly forever. I had been a Labour Party member since the mid-1960s and an active member in Hornsey, York and Uxbridge. So I quickly became involved in Croydon, becoming Chair of the Croydon South constituency and the Local Government Committee, a school governor and a member of the body that in those days served as a patient 'watchdog' in the local NHS, the Community Health Council.

I never wished to become a councillor: my work kept me too busy and I somehow felt that I had imbibed enough local government via my father. In 1984, nevertheless, a Conservative councillor in Croydon's Sanderstead ward, Richard Manchester, resigned his seat (in protest at Mrs Thatcher's callousness) and I was persuaded to stand. It was a hopeless ward for Labour, but one where we could test out new ideas. Younger members in Croydon were breathing new life into the local Party at the time and advocating new campaigning techniques. In particular, those working for the Trade Union Support Unit, funded by the Greater London Council, led the way. So we went for it with gusto. We canvassed extensively, got window bills displayed and brought in numerous activists. Michael Foot, Labour's former leader, joined the campaign and a red double-decker bus toured the leafy streets, much to the surprise of local residents. The result was, even so, a foregone conclusion.

*Sanderstead By-Election Result, 14 November 1984*

| Party | Candidate | Votes |
|-------|-----------|-------|
| Conservative | Peter Stuart GILL | 1889 |
| SDP/Liberal | Christopher PEACOCK | 826 |
| Labour | Malcolm WICKS | 448 |

## An unsuspected family connection

I decided that I should seek to become Labour's candidate in the forthcoming 1987 General Election in Croydon North-West. We lived in the south of the borough and I could not claim to know its northern wards very well. Some key activists there knew me, but many others did not. As one rival put it: "Just because Malcolm's written a couple of books, that doesn't mean he should become the candidate!" While my wife's parents came originally from the area (which was why the borough became our base for looking for a new house) I imagined I had no previous connection with Croydon. Only years later, thanks to the work of my Parliamentary Assistant, Louise Szpera, did I learn that there had been members of my family living in Croydon's Old Town. Louise, whose hobby is genealogy, discovered past family members who lived in the town when it had a population of only around 6,000. They had been baptised, married and in many cases buried at Croydon Parish Church. My great, great, great, great grandfather, Philip Wicks, his wife and young family arrived in Croydon at the end of the 18th century. Philip was to end his days in the Union Workhouse at Duppas Hill, reminding us that most people's ancestors were poor and that the poor law loomed over many lives. His son, Edward, worked as a cowman and gardener, before entering the Whitgift Almshouses around 1871 with his wife, Jane, where they were to remain for over 20 years. Edward boosted his weekly income of 10 shillings [50p] plus £3.10s-quarterly, by £1 per quarter through undertaking the additional duties as:

> ...porter and for ringing the Chapel Bell, taking the front gates of (sic) the hinges and pushing them on again morning and night. Locking the front door every night and unlocking every morning. Keeping the ash pit clean and occasionally sweeping the pavement[23].

This he continued to do well into his 80s. However, by 1911 the Wicks family had moved to inner London and the first Wicks to live in Islington, where my father was brought up, was my great grandfather, William Frederick Wicks.

## Garnering support

In my quest for the Croydon North West nomination, my main problem was that the 'Hard Left' had a strong footing in the constituency. A few supporters of the Trotskyist Militant Tendency were also part of the fray. Indeed, I recall how a year or so earlier, in the pub after a meeting, a young Militant activist had tried to recruit me to the 'entryist' tendency, whose revolutionary aims had already been declared incompatible with those of the Labour Party. I replied that I would join if I could become leader. Displaying the characteristic humour by-pass of many extremists, the young man stared at me blankly.

The selection process then in place (which has since been abandoned in favour of 'one member, one vote') was ultimately down to the General Management Committee (GMC), a body of some 30-

40 delegates representing six local branches and other affiliated bodies, mainly trade unions. The only chance of getting on to the final shortlist was if you had received nominations from local branches. This involved meeting the local members and competing for their support. My most dispiriting experience of this ritual was the Norbury branch. Three of us would-be candidates were in competition and only six members of the branch had turned up to vote. It was held in someone's flat and when I was called in to speak, I spotted a young activist who was looking at me like something the proverbial cat had brought in. The walls of the flat were thin and after we had all spoken and the votes had been cast, I could hear the Chair reporting the results. I had come bottom with just one vote. The other two were level and there had to be a second round of voting. But not before I had learned through the wall that: "We might as well tell Malcolm to go home!"

On the way back to South Croydon by double-decker bus I was gloom personified: "Why am I doing this? It's so awful and undignified!" But I did pick up nominations (from wiser branches!) and headed, with my rivals, for the all-important final selection meeting. Here, I was at a serious disadvantage. Hugh Atkinson, a hard-working and serious 'hard' left activist, was way out ahead as favourite. He was Secretary of the local Party and a member of the Bensham Manor Branch, which was regularly attended by over 30 members. He lived in the constituency and I didn't. The GMC delegates included many from the 'hard' left and, while I considered myself as on the 'democratic' left of the Party, I had never had any truck with this faction. To stand any chance of winning – and six or so of us were up for selection – I had to hope Hugh would not win outright in the first round and that I could pick up votes as others dropped out. Essentially, I had to pick up every non-hard left vote, plus any others who, for whatever reason, were not automatically supporting Hugh.

As a would-be candidate, you never really know how things are going on these occasions until the announcement. My speech went OK, and I think I dealt with questions pretty well too. It was then a matter of waiting, for what seemed like an interminable time. Rather to everyone's surprise, I won by 16 votes to 14. There were all sorts of recriminations, reactions and rumours after the meeting. Later, I discovered the real reason why I had won. One woman delegate became angry when the female candidate she was supporting was knocked out in an early round of voting. She told me later:

> *Damn it, if they want another middle-aged, middle-class, white male, I might as well vote for Malcolm!*

She also confided that her, then, partner had voted for me because I was the only candidate who made him laugh. Thus, my ambition to become a prospective Parliamentary candidate was achieved, not by the clarity of my vision for democratic social change or my devastating critique of Thatcherism, but through being perceived as the least obnoxious male candidate with a sense of humour.

### Robin Cook and a case of mistaken identity

The Labour Party was anxious to support its prospective Parliamentary candidates in a variety of ways. We attended regular sessions at the House of Commons where Shadow Cabinet Ministers spoke to us and we talked through issues and campaigning methods. There was a regular photo opportunity and during one session in 1986/7, this was with Neil Kinnock. The candidates queued up just off Westminster Hall. I was chatting to fellow candidates when the late Robin Cook[24] took me by the arm and said that he needed an urgent word.

We went into one of the rooms. He said: "You do realise, don't you, that you won't be able to have your photo taken with Neil?" I was speechless for a few seconds, no doubt trying to recall what terrible misdemeanour I had committed. "But why?" I eventually asked. Devastatingly, Robin replied: "You work for News International!" Here I should explain that this was taking place during the Wapping dispute when Rupert Murdoch had opened a new, non-unionised production plant for his newspapers and the trade unions were besieging it. I told Robin that I certainly did not work for News International, but he still persisted "You're a *Sun* journalist!"

Such was Robin's authority and intensity that it almost occurred to me that I might actually be a *Sun* reporter and had somehow forgotten. He eventually believed my explanation that I was the Director of the Family Policy Studies Centre and had nothing to do with the Murdoch empire. It turned out to be a case of mistaken identity and that another candidate was the 'culprit'.

Whether or not I would have become a parliamentary candidate if I had been unsuccessful in Croydon I cannot say. It would have been difficult and, in any case, I never envied the dual lives of Parliamentary colleagues who served constituencies far away from London, often separated from their families for over half the week.

*General Election 1987*

I am, however, getting ahead of myself, since my becoming a Labour candidate for the 1987 General Election – Mrs Thatcher's second landslide – was not by any means the same thing as becoming a Member of Parliament. The campaign in Croydon North West was, nevertheless, an extraordinarily exciting experience for me as a new candidate. It was also one of the most exhausting experiences of my life. For a somewhat unusual reason, the Labour Party started the race in third place. This was because, in 1981, a by-election had taken place following the death of the Conservative MP, Robert Taylor. In normal circumstances the by-election would have been a straight fight between Conservative and Labour (although the Labour Party had never actually won the seat). But in March 1981, the breakaway Social Democratic Party (SDP) was riding high, led by its 'gang of four' former Labour Ministers – Roy Jenkins, Shirley Williams, Bill Rodgers and David Owen. There was some talk that Shirley Williams might fight the by-election for the new Alliance formed between the SDP and the Liberals. But in the event, Bill Pitt of the Liberal Party, who had fought the seat on the three previous occasions, became their standard-bearer. The by-election result was a spectacular victory for Bill Pitt, who beat the Conservative candidate, John Butterfill, by over 3,000 votes. However, at the 1983 General Election the Conservatives regained the seat. Humfrey Malins was elected MP, but with Bill Pitt, in second place, some way ahead of Labour.

So, as we approached the 1987 campaign, we were hardly favourites. Yet we fought a fantastically energetic and well-resourced campaign, not least thanks to our young organiser, David Evans. Several trade union officials came in to lend support for the duration of the campaign and we had large numbers of activists. We easily out-numbered the Tories in the number of window bills. Indeed, we worked so hard that at some stage I think we felt we had to win. Yet some days before election day, having looked at our own canvass returns, we knew that we were not going to make it. Following a frantic polling day, where we did our utmost to get every vote out, the count took place and the results were duly declared.

*1987 General Election Result, Croydon North West*

| Party | Candidate | Votes | % | +/-% |
|-------|-----------|-------|---|------|
| Conservative | Humfrey MALINS | 18,665 | 47.0 | 4.7 |
| Labour | Malcolm WICKS | 14,677 | 37.0 | 12.8 |
| Liberal | L A ROWE | 6,363 | 16.0 | -15.9 |
| | **Majority** | 3,988 | 10.0 | |
| | **Turnout** | 39,705 | | |

The good news was that we were back in second place and that our vote had increased significantly. Indeed, the swing to Labour – 12.7 per cent – was one of the highest in the country. But we had still lost.

# 8.

# *On Becoming an MP*

The General Election result five years later, in April 1992, was a tale of mixed fortunes and mixed emotions. I had won and fulfilled my ambition to be an MP. After another vigorously fought campaign in the constituency, re-named Croydon North, there was a further swing to Labour that was, this time, enough to take the seat.

*1992 General Election Result, Croydon North*

| Party | Candidate | Votes | % | +/-% |
|---|---|---|---|---|
| Labour | Malcolm WICKS | 19,153 | 47.3 | +10.3 |
| Conservative | Humfrey MALINS | 17,626 | 43.5 | -3.5 |
| Liberal Democrat | Mrs L F HAWKINS | 3,728 | 9.2 | --6.8 |
| | **Majority** | 1,527 | 3.8 | -6.3 |
| | **Turnout** | 40,507 | | |

But nationally, the Party had lost – yet again – following our defeats in 1979, 1983 and 1987. Neil Kinnock, a leader I admired (who had been maligned mercilessly during the campaign by Rupert Murdoch's *Sun* newspaper) would never be Prime Minister. I wrote an emotional letter to Neil urging him to fight on, but I was being unrealistic.

## Learning the ropes

After polling day, there was a delay before the House of Commons was summoned. It was a time to relax and to celebrate with local supporters at the victory party in Croydon's trade union and Labour headquarters, Ruskin House. Still gloomy at Labour's overall defeat, I was in no hurry to rush up to the House, knowing that the allocation of offices took an interminable age. But my friend Andrew MacKinlay, the new Labour MP for Thurrock, phoned and was unimpressed that I had not immediately headed up to Westminster. "You must get your locker key!", he advised. And indeed, with no office for several weeks let alone other office facilities, the locker was useful. This was notwithstanding the fact that for perhaps the last 15 years of my Parliamentary career I never used the locker at all. I had lost the key – and sometimes suspected that there might still be an antique cheese sandwich lurking behind the locker door.

I think that by 1992, the House of Commons was beginning to go through a transition to something more modern. But it was sometimes difficult to see this. A man with enormous power in the Parliamentary Labour Party was Ray Powell, the MP for Ogmore and the Whip who allocated offices. The conversation, when I approached him about the possibilities, was succinct:

*"So you'd like an office?"*

*"Yes, please".*

*"Right, put it in writing".*

Ray was a decent man, but he was not one to wear his power lightly. There was, in any case, a supposed shortage of rooms. So Hugh

Bayley, the new MP for York, and I agreed to share what turned out to be a good-sized office. The deal was that I would bring a kettle and he would stop smoking (which, as a health economist, he knew he should be doing anyway).

One of my first impressions of the House of Commons (and this is far from being an original observation) was that it resembled a boarding school, albeit that you were normally allowed to go home at night. Maybe it was the grandeur of the buildings themselves; maybe it was the distinction between the new boys (and some girls) and the older lags. Perhaps, too, it was the presence of the 'prefects' like Ray Powell; albeit they were known as Whips. It certainly took a while to learn the ropes. One day I was in the House of Commons gym and had just entered the shower when, to my dismay, the division bell rang. I had just minutes to get dry and pull my gym kit back on to race over to the Chamber to vote. Two veteran Tory MPs, very much from the 'squirearchy', looked me up and down and I heard one murmur, sotto voce: "Standards are falling."

---

### Backing Bryan Gould for leader

After our defeat in the 1992 election an early challenge for the Labour Party was to elect a new leader. John Smith, the MP for North Lanarkshire, was the lead contender and had massive support in the party. I, however, supported Bryan Gould, a New Zealander by birth and the MP for Dagenham. I had been attracted by his intellectual input into Labour's thinking. I soon attracted a phone call from Robin Cook, acting as John Smith's campaign manager. I regarded Robin as a very formidable politician. He said words to the effect that having looked at who was supporting John and who was supporting Bryan he was surprised to see my name on the wrong list! He asked for an explanation and I did my best to give him one.

As a newly-elected MP, I decided to establish a shop-front constituency office in Croydon North in a prime location. I thought it important that voters could see that I meant business in terms of the service and advice that I could offer them. I was determined not to be an aloof Member of Parliament, as some still were and many had been in the past. Stories abound of MPs over the years who would put a notice in the local paper that they would be visiting their constituency on such and such a date – sometimes months after their last visit – as if this somehow epitomised what a good constituency MP should be doing. The office location improved over the years, as did the House of Commons allowance for staffing. This meant that, eventually, three caseworkers could be employed to deal with the many demands and pressures in a constituency with a large electorate that reflected the increasing cultural diversity of Croydon.

Although Alison Butler, my Constituency Office Manager, and her team took much of the routine pressure away from me, I held regular advice surgeries on a weekly basis. The advice surgeries (and those who came to see me) covered the most extraordinary range of subjects: some relatively trivial (such as a contested parking ticket) and some that could not have been more tragic. Croydon was not immune from gang warfare and one of the hardest things was to sit down with the parents of a murdered teenager, stabbed to death, to listen to their heartache and search my mind for something practical that I could do to help them.

From the start, I found that another of the most difficult things confronting a constituency MP – along with many other frontline staff – was mental ill health. How do you treat the mentally ill constituent equally, and with dignity, even when it becomes apparent to you that they are very ill? I remember once gently advising a man that he should talk to his doctor, who rejected the suggestion: "He thinks I'm mad, Mr Wicks, he's no help." I also soon discovered how difficult many people find it to draw a line and move on following an incident, setback, or complaint that the authorities cannot deal with adequately.

It becomes clear that this is what they need to do, but it is still extremely hard for them.

## Labour Friends of Bosnia

Internationally, during my first term as an MP, one of the most disturbing and intractable situations was the mounting tension, ethnic conflict and bloodshed in the former Yugoslavia, and especially in Bosnia-Herzegovina. This was complex territory, and not just in terms of terrain. But one thing was clear enough: Sarajevo, the Bosnian capital, was surrounded by forces under the political control of Radovan Karadžić, the leader of Bosnia's minority Serbian community, supported by the Belgrade regime of the Serbian President, Slobodan Milošević. Innocent citizens were being killed on a daily basis and the world, including the UK government, was reluctant to act.

International relations had never been my speciality. Indeed a Parliamentary colleague said at the time: "We expected Malcolm to talk a lot about the welfare state, so why is he so obsessed with Bosnia?" I admit that I initially struggled to find Bosnia on the map! But I still felt that something truly catastrophic was unfolding there. I guess, in my heart, that I was what is nowadays termed, a 'liberal interventionist'; believing that if you have the power to act, you simply do not walk by on the other side. A group of us on the Labour backbenches decided to meet, in one of the small rooms off Westminster Hall, and we were surprised by how many turned up. We decided to initiate the Labour Friends of Bosnia (LFB). Our aims were to highlight the issue in Parliament and, more publicly, to urge the case for intervention. To be blunt, we also wanted to kick the Labour frontbench into action. The Parliamentary Labour Party in general was not exactly covering itself in glory; indeed, several MPs were members of an All-Party Group with close ties to the Belgrade regime. In a leaflet announcing the formation of Labour Friends of Bosnia, our objectives were detailed as follows:

*Labour Friends of Bosnia has been established to mobilise support across the Labour Movement for a plural, multi-ethnic, democratic Bosnia, and to oppose by all means necessary the attempt to create ethnic apartheid in the Balkans.*

LFB supports:

- *robust enforcement by UNPROFOR[25] of the UN Mandate to deliver humanitarian aid and to protect safe areas. Any attempt to thwart the execution of these mandates should be met with force.*
- *all practical material assistance and moral support to the Government of Bosnia, commensurate with international law, to recreate a multi-ethnic, open, plural and democratic political community over the whole of Bosnia-Herzegovina.*

*The Government's policy is based upon callous expediency and appeasement: Labour's must be based on principles and values. Fifty years after the defeat of Hitler, a quarter of a million people have died in another ethnic holocaust in Europe. The international community has the means to stop it. What it lacks is the political will. The Labour Party in Britain, and the forces of democratic socialism across Europe, must now supply it.*

Around this time, I and fellow founder-members of the LFB, Kate Hoey[26] and Calum MacDonald[27], encountered Tony Blair, then Shadow Home Secretary, waiting in the Members Lobby in between votes. We expressed our misgivings about Labour's frontbench position. "Yeah," he replied, "We're not in the right place on this one are we?"

*A visit to Sarajevo*

In the autumn of 1993, Calum MacDonald received a message from the US Democrat Congressman and campaigner, Frank McCloskey, saying that he and other international parliamentarians were hoping to visit Sarajevo in October. Kate Hoey and I quickly agreed to go with Calum. However, the US Military, and even more so the British authorities, were nervous and became uncooperative about our travel plans. We decided to fly to Zagreb in Croatia to meet up with the rest of the delegation consisting of two Malaysian parliamentarians, an Australian, a Scandinavian, an Italian Member of the European Parliament and two US Congressmen. The next interesting problem was how to fly into Sarajevo itself. There was much kerfuffle over this with, apparently, one General vetoing our proposed visit, and another over-ruling him. We flew into Sarajevo on a Russian plane under the command of UNPROFOR[28]. Armoured personnel carriers [APCs] took us to the Presidential Palace where we met Bosnia's President Izetbegovic, parliamentarians and others, followed by a press conference.

Despite the initial efforts made to thwart our plan to visit Sarajevo, once it was clear that we were bound to Sarajevo, the US embassy produced all sorts of security equipment for the two US Congressmen and their staff; flak jackets, helmets and the rest. Did the British authorities swing into similar action, thinking to themselves that although they didn't want the MPs to go, they had better give them some basic protection? Did they hell...

It was always the intention of Calum, Kate and myself to stay in Sarajevo for a few days after the rest of the international delegation departed. UNPROFOR knew our plans, but I think it is fair to say that they tried to trick us into going home on an earlier flight. They insisted it would be easier from a security point of view if the whole delegation went to Sarajevo airport, after which arrangements could be made for we three MPs. Sure enough, at the airport they tried to get us on to the plane heading for Zagreb. There was quite a confrontation. They asked how we would get back to Sarajevo. I replied that the UN should provide transport, but if necessary we would walk.

(A slightly absurd image presents itself of us hiking down 'bomb alley'). Calum wrote in his contemporary account of events that:

*"Malcolm brings his poshest voice and the most diplomatic manner to bear."*

However, the star of the show was Kate as she engaged in a no-holds-barred, verbal set-to with a French Major. He was tough, muscular and chock-full with guns and ammunition. But he was no match for Kate and we were duly driven back to Sarajevo to spend the next day looking round the city, seeing the devastation for ourselves, observing the danger zones, meeting local people and witnessing their bravery and dignity in the face of truly enormous tragedy.

We stayed, as did so many journalists, at the Holiday Inn. Luxury it was not. It was cold and gloomy and largely empty. Most windows were blasted out. At night you could hear the shells fired from Serbian positions around the city continuing to fall. Only the first couple of floors of the hotel could be occupied. Black plastic sheets covered the windows to protect the residents from snipers. We were fortunate to have contacts living in the city and others, including journalists covering the war, who were pleased to show us around and introduce us to local people. Shortly after I returned to England, I wrote up an account of one such meeting for my local Croydon paper and I hope it still captures the atmosphere in Sarajevo during the few days that we were there:

*Aida and her family were grateful for our visit. They insisted on opening the last bottle of white wine for us, we ate pumpkin pie and it could have been a scene from any European town.*

*In many respects still, Sarajevo is a town like ours. But the similarities fade each time a shell thuds into the shattered streets. Aida is now a student, but she has been an interpreter for British journalists covering the war.*

*Recently a mortar exploded near the room where she liked to sit* and the force of it propelled her across the house. She was uninjured, but on another occasion her sister, Anela, was not so lucky: she suffered a leg wound.

Their mother's sister was killed recently and the family business, a hairdressing salon, was destroyed by a shell. Life is grim: there is no water in homes, toilets cannot be flushed, and there is pitifully little food. There is no electricity and the Serbs have cut off the natural gas supply.

It was the most beautifully cooked pumpkin pie, but we ate it guiltily, yet knowing that the wish to give hospitality outweighed their need to conserve supplies.

Just one family, but a glimpse into the hell that is now Bosnia.

On the day we flew in we were driven into the city in UN APCs – Armoured Personnel Carriers – and we were told it had been a 'quiet day'. When we visited Kosovo hospital, we discovered what that meant – by 3pm two dead and seven wounded.

That day 149 shells were to fall on Sarajevo and like any day people walk the streets knowing that the snipers in the surrounding hills, and in the buildings occupied by the Serbs, could be targeting them through the telescopic sights of their sophisticated weaponry. All have friends or family who have been killed since this brutal conflict began.

The hospital could have been Mayday[29] – modern, with good equipment and staff. But it now battles against the odds.

Yet the work – crucial work in war – continues. Many operations are being undertaken with help from visiting specialists from Europe, including Britain.

In the summer operations were being done by torchlight and candle and there is often no power to run vital equipment, including X-rays.

But atrocity is no respecter of hospitals and Kosovo had suffered 183 direct hits since the start of the war: the dead included four doctors. All around we saw shell damage, while inside a man shot while queuing for bread was being treated.

*In the face of the bombardment of Sarajevo, which has intensified again in recent days, the people have shown enormous courage, dignity and defiance.*

*Increasingly people seek to maintain as near a normal life as is humanly possible. For too long they had to cower, now they shop, albeit for little, walk and talk in the streets of their city, even though they know that the next bullet might be for them.*

*The designation of Sarajevo as a UN-protected 'safe area' and the de-escalation of shelling since August, has created an unjustifiable complacency on the part of Western governments.*

*The siege of attrition goes on, regardless of Sarajevo's protected status. The UN is being treated with contempt by the Serb forces. No diesel has reached the city since August. There is no gas, no tap water, and no electricity.*

*The UN has a minimum survival ration target of 600 grams per person per day, but currently is only able to deliver and distribute 200-300 grams per person. Supplies of shelter equipment, vital for the winter months, have hardly started to arrive.*

*Sarajevo is a modern European city, not some faraway place. One scene will always remain sketched on my memory, as the sharpest contrast between past hope and current fear, between good and evil.*

*To the left, we saw the indoor stadium for the 1984 Winter Olympics, now gutted and burnt, to the right a new cemetery, created for the dead of recent months.*

*On one side, then, the memory of Ravel's Bolero, Torvill and Dean skating to gold: on the other, a war and slaughter.*

*We are heading towards an humanitarian disaster this winter. People are thinner and weaker than last year. Now all the wood is gone, including much domestic furniture which has been chopped for firewood. Aida's family showed us the furniture already destined to be burned.*

*The UN workers and soldiers on the ground are working their hearts out but they have been let down by Western governments, particularly by members of the Security Council.*

*The mandate for delivering aid is clearly inadequate. The breakaway Serbs can delay and restrict the aid arriving at will, as well as subjecting the city to continuous sniper and shell fire as we ourselves witnessed.*

*The West faces a stark choice if disaster is to be avoided. One option is for the existing airlift to be massively increased to bring in enough food, fuel and shelter to allow the population to survive. The alternative is to change UNPROFOR's mandate to allow aid to be forced through by road.*

## *An audience with* Dr Karadžić

On our last day in Bosnia, we ensured our visit ended on an even deeper note of disquiet – if that were possible – by meeting Radovan Karadžić at his headquarters in the outlying town of Pale. It has to be admitted we had arranged the meeting with the Serbian leader in an unusual way. We simply informed the UNPROFOR officers who were, reluctantly, keeping an eye on us that Dr Karadžić had agreed to meet us. This was, I'm afraid, a piece of creative fiction. We asked for transport to get to Pale, but we had no idea if any would be provided.

On our final evening in Sarajevo we enjoyed a wonderful dinner with the journalists and photographers that we had got to know, and we must have returned to the Holiday Inn quite late. So it was something of a shock when at six o'clock the next morning we got a message that an armoured personnel carrier was waiting for us downstairs, and would be leaving in ten minutes. A tall order on any morning, but the electricity was down, the bathroom had no natural lighting and there was just a trickle of water from the tap. Somehow we made it downstairs and found ourselves heading to Pale for a meeting that hadn't really been arranged. This, too, I described in my article for the local paper:

*On our final day we had a meeting with Dr Karadži , the leader of the Bosnian Serbs. We met him with grave misgivings, but were determined to put direct to him the questions that have been on the minds of many in Britain.*

*Before our meeting, having journeyed to his HQ in Pale, with the UN, we were talking to two UN monitoring officers when there was a very loud explosion, loud enough for the two officers to run outside to investigate. They concluded that it was a shell fired from close by in the direction of Sarajevo.*

*Our first question to Dr Karadži was obvious: why do you continue to bombard the city, despite the ceasefire?*

*He denied that there was any shelling. But what about the shell that we ourselves had just heard being fired? 'I will investigate immediately', he said and made a phone call.*

*We had witnessed the strange world of Dr Karadži where fact and fiction, reality and fantasy, are blurred.*

*Later I asked him why his forces had pursued the terrible practice of 'ethnic cleansing', including the mass rape of Muslim women. He said categorically that 'the Serbs did not do atrocities'. As for mass rapes, this was a 'complete lie'. I said that these had been well-documented by some of our newspapers' most reliable journalists. 'No this is a lie', he asserted.*

*And so our meeting was characterised by this denial of truths.*

*'Why not stop the siege?' Answer: 'We don't keep a siege'.*

*As we drove back to Sarajevo we hoped that the interview we had just given on TV, where we spoke clearly about our views, would not be shown on Serbian TV before we got through Serbian checkpoints and back to Sarajevo!*[30]

A less serious recollection from our sojourn into "the strange world of Dr Karadži " was passing time before the meeting with a Danish UNPROFOR soldier who was there to monitor developments. He was listening to the Scottish band *Runrig* and turned out to be a big fan of Celtic rock. Later he played Mark Knopfler's 'Going Home', the theme music from the film *Local Hero*. It turned out that both Calum and I had used it as our election campaign theme tune.

There was one person who was far from impressed by my statements about Bosnia, and that was my father. As noted earlier (See Chapter 1), he was a conscientious objector during the Second World War and had not changed his position. He heard me on an early morning radio news programme advocating intervention. I was in my constituency office doing my advice surgery later when he phoned. "Is that the Minister for War?" was his opening question, and he was not joking. The conversation did not get any easier. I think I said that we would have to agree to differ on this important point.

Labour Friends of Bosnia attracted the support of over 60 backbenchers and also activists in the party at large. Michael Foot and his wife, Jill Craigie, were our Presidents. Clare Short[31] was the Chair and I acted as a convenor alongside Kate Hoey and Calum MacDonald. Among our members were the MPs Tony Banks, Hugh Bayley, John Denham, Angela Eagle, Frank Field, Peter Hain, Keith Hill, Margaret Hodge, Ken Livingstone, Chris Mullin, Giles Radice, Nick Raynsford, Clive Soley, Stephen Timms and Tony Wright.

Although I think the weight of Labour backbench opinion was largely content with the Shadow Cabinet's line, which seemed to involve keeping about one progressive step ahead of the Foreign Office Ministers, Douglas Hurd and Douglas Hogg, we had, nevertheless, assembled a gathering of able, intelligent and thoughtful dissenters. It was good to have this support in the Parliamentary Labour Party at a time when some MPs appeared to be in open alliance with the Serbian side. One Labour front bench spokesman apparently telephoned Karadži on a regular basis. "I've just been speaking to Radovan," he told a fellow MP in the division lobby, seeking to persuade my colleague that the Doctor was a reasonable man. Both Michael Foot and Jill Craigie, were particularly staunch in their opposition to appeasement and it was good to have such authoritative backing for our campaign. I recall visiting their home in Pilgrims Lane in Hampstead. They decided to make a documentary about the crisis, which later appeared as *Two Hours from London*. I was interviewed for the film and described a 3am session in Parliament when Edward Heath, the former Tory leader, great European and powerful supporter of the Common Market, was to be heard unaccountably pleading with the Prime Minister, John Major, not to intervene in Bosnia. As I said in the film: "A huge murmur arose in the House of Commons – mainly on the government benches, but I am sorry to say partly on the opposition benches too – and I thought that's it; that's the murmur of Munich".

9.

# *The Carers Act 1995*

While the vast majority of legislation is property of the Government – introduced by the executive and carried through the Commons by the ruling Party majority – there are exceptions. The most important are Private Members' Bills, which enable a few lucky backbench MPs to introduce their own legislation. But it is a procedure fraught with difficulty. The crucial necessary ingredient is time: time to get the Bill introduced in the Commons, time to get into the Committee Stage to discuss the provision in detail and then time for the House of Lords to complete its own deliberations. Few backbench bills survive this long and tortuous process.

In each parliamentary session a ballot is held for backbenchers wishing to bid for the chance to introduce their own bill. If they draw a high number in this parliamentary lottery they will be able to introduce the Second Reading of their chosen bill first thing on a Friday morning, which is normally a very quiet day in the Commons reserved for backbench business. Two days are set aside in one of the division lobbies for those wishing to enter the ballot. They are required to place their signature by a chosen number in a special ledger – the equivalent of choosing a raffle ticket. Joining the short queue in 1994, I was struck by just how seriously some MPs negotiated this task. They would look for their lucky number – their wife's birthday? their Parliamentary majority perhaps? who knows? – hoping it had not already been pinched by another MP. My approach was more mundane: I simply signed against the first space that caught my eye.

I then rather forgot all about it until my office suddenly began to be inundated with calls, faxes and the rest, all beseeching, demanding, even begging me to introduce a particular legislative measure. From this I deduced that I had won a reasonably high place in the ballot. In fact, I had drawn number 11; not bad, though not quite high enough to guarantee me first slot on a Friday morning. What I had 'won' was the right to go second. As it turned out, this was not an insuperable obstacle, but one that required some nifty footwork.

I had not gone into the ballot process with legislation already drafted and tucked under my arm. The odds against succeeding in the ballot made that an unwise precaution. I know MPs who have been in the Commons for over 20 years without once coming anywhere near to introducing their own legislation. So for the time being I became very popular. All sorts of lobbies, voluntary organisations, business and professional bodies had a bill they wanted to promote and were anxious to beat an urgent path to my door. Some I gave short shrift to. One lobby, which included business, told me how they would write to all my constituents, should I introduce their Bill saying what a wonderful MP I was. I showed them the door. In the end, the choice I had to make was between two Bills that were both very close to my heart and interests. The first concerned energy efficiency and home insulation: things I was deeply committed to following my 1970s research on hypothermia (see Chapter 4). However, the legislative project I eventually chose, concerned carers: the estimated six million or so family members and others who were providing unpaid care for spouses and partners, children and others. This related to my work at the Family Policy Studies Centre (see Chapter 6) and, in particular a report, *The Forgotten Army*, that I wrote with Melanie Henwood. In that study, for the first time, we calculated the notional value of care, using the best estimates available at the time of the numbers of carers (this was before any national data on carers existed) and the hours they spent in caring each week. We estimated that the annual value of such care was somewhere between £3.7 and £5.3 billion. Such figures seem highly conservative now but need to be seen in context; comparative public expenditure data from the time indicated £928 millions spent annually on social services for people aged 75 and over, and £3.9 billions being accounted for in total health and social services expenditure on this population. The notional value of informal care provided substantive evidence on the sheer importance of the caring role of families, and provided a powerful argument for increasing support for carers who for too long had been the Welfare State's 'forgotten army'[32].

It was the Carers National Association (CNA) – now known as Carers UK – who lobbied me to introduce the Bill. Their Director was the impressive Jill Pitkeathley, whom I knew well. She and her colleagues provided me with expert backup and lobbying resources, with their Deputy Director, Francine Bates, taking specific responsibility for co-ordination. There can be different motivations on the part of a backbencher when introducing a Bill into the Commons. One is to herald a great campaign to achieve a very substantial reform. I think back to the long campaign to abolish capital punishment, which involved numerous Private Members' Bills and the zealous determination of Sydney Silverman MP before it succeeded. Another motivation is more practical – to get legislation straight on to the statute book, however modest a start it may provide. This was the route I chose.

Prior to what became my Carers (Recognition and Services) Act of 1995, policy in the area of improving the support available for carers had been sparse. But the increased attention paid to the issue by the research and academic communities through the 1980s and 1990s certainly raised its profile. Politicians increasingly paid lip service to such matters, but there was a need to move beyond rhetoric to practical support. Community care policy at the time was based on the proposals contained in a policy White Paper *Caring for People* in 1989 that had been enacted in 1990[33]. One of the six key objectives espoused by the original policy document was:

*...to ensure that service providers make practical support for carers a high priority.* (paragraph 1.11).

Furthermore, in assessing people's needs for care and support, social services departments were advised that:

*Assessments should take account of the wishes of the individual and his or her carer, and of the carer's ability to continue to provide care, and where possible should include their active participation.* (Paragraph 3.2.6)

This expectation was not, however, specified in the NHS and Community Care Act 1990. Accompanying guidance issued to local authorities by the Department of Health advised that carers should be able to ask for a separate assessment; but it was evident that, in practice, most carers were not being adequately recognised, nor benefiting from an assessment of their own needs. My Bill was designed to give statutory backing to carers, entitlement to an assessment of their own and for local authorities to provide services to meet carers' needs when assessed.

*Finding cross-party support*

I knew I could only succeed if I attracted cross-party support for my Bill and crucially obtained the support, or at least the acquiescence of the Conservative Government. Fortunately, our campaign had a great deal going for it. The carers issue was receiving more media prominence and I secured, with the help from the CNA, a formidable line-up of cross-party sponsors for my Bill. They included Alan Howarth (Con), Archy Kirkwood (Lib Dem), Margaret Ewing (SNP), the Rev Martin Smyth (Ulster Unionist) and Dafydd Wigley (Plaid Cymru).

The first draft was drawn up with support from the House of Commons Clerks Department. It was very much a work in progress and once we got into discussions it needed extensive redrafting. But it was a start. The Bill made its first appearance in *Hansard*, the official House of Commons record, as follows:

*Mr. Malcolm Wicks, supported by Mr. Hugh Bayley, Mr. Roger Berry, Mr. Tom Clarke, Mrs. Margaret Ewing, Mr. Frank Field, Mr. Alan Howarth, Ms Tessa Jowell, Mr. Archy Kirkwood, Rev. Martin Smyth, Ms Rachel Squire and Mr. Dafydd Wigley, presented a Bill to provide for the assessment of the needs of carers and for the provision of services to them by social services authorities; and to amend the law relating to the definition of the term "private carer": And the same was read the First time; and ordered to be read a Second time upon 3 March, and to be printed. [Bill 17.]* [34]

The Secretary of State for Health at the time was Virginia Bottomley, someone who had, fortunately, long been associated with the carers' movement. As hoped, we were able to secure her broad support. But next it was a question of detailed negotiation with her Department of Health officials and her junior Minister, John Bowis, the Parliamentary Under-Secretary of State. Here, too, we were fortunate; he could not have been more sympathetic. We did, nevertheless, encounter one difficult moment with the civil servants over the question of young carers. These are children who find themselves, in the difficult position of having to look after a chronically sick or disabled relative. At a critical meeting an official from the children's division of the Department of Health came along determined to tell me – and, more critically, the Minister – why young carers should not be included in the Bill. The attempted justification revealed bureaucratic boundaries at their worst:

*This matter concerns children's legislation and should not be confused with carers and community care!*

We argued our corner, with the Minister listening carefully. Finally I lost patience: "Forget departmental division and legislative boundaries," I said. "These children *are* carers and there is increasing concern about their plight." I then played what I hoped would be my ace. Looking directly at John Bowis, and glancing around at his officials, I declared that it would be impossible for the Minister to stand up in the Commons and deny child carers a place in the legislation. I could see that he agreed with me and that we had won on that one.


*A race against time*


The real battle, however, lay ahead and the battlefield was not one determined by government but by Parliament. It was about winning time for the passage of the Bill and, of course, winning Commons approval. As explained, I had not come quite high enough in the ballot to introduce the Second Reading of my Bill first thing on a Friday morning – the coveted pole position. This meant things started to get difficult because the first Bill being introduced on the allocated day (3rd March 1995) was the anti-hunting Wild Mammals (Protection) Bill sponsored by John McFall MP. Nothing could have been more controversial at that time, with the 'tally-ho' brigade out to oppose the proposed ban and in full cry. The day turned out to be a cliff-hanger. The Wild Mammals Bill debate started at 9.41am and finally received its second reading at 2.19pm after a vote.

Then it was my turn and the timing was now critical. Commons rules dictated that if any Member was still speaking after 2.30pm the Bill would be deemed to have been 'talked out'. So my long speech was discarded. We had just a few minutes for my own speech and for the Minister to give his reply. Rachel Squire, the MP for Dunfermline West, was sitting next to me, ready to tug me down by my jacket should I show any danger of misreading the clock. So all my research, all my knowledge and my passion for the subject came down to this remarkably short speech:

> *I beg to move, That the Bill be now read a Second time.*
>
> *As time is limited, I want to be sure that I give the Minister time to respond. The Bill is supported by the Carers National Association and by many prominent charities and voluntary organisations. I believe that it has and deserves the support of the House.*
>
> *The aims of the Bill are, first, to give carers—many caring around the clock for people with Alzheimer's disease and other serious conditions—the right to have their own needs assessed by local authorities. Secondly, it will enable those local authorities to have the power to provide support and services. I am sure that all hon. Members who have met carers know that many of them are in desperate need of that support.*
>
> *I am grateful to the Under-Secretary of State for Health for the way in which we have been able to engage in positive discussions with both him and with civil servants. None of us wishes to play politics with carers; this is an opportunity for the House as a whole to show its support, regard and recognition for carers.*
>
> *Politicians often call for greater responsibility among families and citizens. I believe that the carers of Britain, who number 6.8 million, are among the most responsible citizens in this country. If politicians condemn irresponsibility from time to time, they must also recognise responsibility. I have been to Northern Ireland, Scotland, Wales and England—including Croydon—and I have met many carers. I have a high regard for them. I am struck by the modesty of their demands, given the immense burden of care that they shoulder on behalf of all of us. They are responsible citizens, who have conducted a highly responsible campaign about their needs.*
>
> *We need one more act of responsibility, and that is for a united House of Commons to make a responsible decision to support the Bill.*[35]

Having sat down, you really do hold your breath; for it takes only one MP to shout, "Object!" for your bill to be effectively killed. And this happens frequently, either from MPs with sincere objections to a proposed measure, or from a small 'awkward squad' of Tory backbenchers who simply object to more legislation, in what they presumably regard as an over-regulated society. On this occasion, the Commons stayed silent and our luck was still in.

## The next stages

While our campaign was making progress, we still had to complete the Bill's main stages in the Commons and then push on into the House of Lords. During this whole period we campaigned vigorously in the country, and through the media, as well as in Parliament. The CNA was my rock and both Jill Pitkeathley and Francine Bates provided solid and enthusiastic support. We kept our eyes firmly on the prize, which was to get onto the statute book the first ever legislation recognising the needs of carers.

I travelled the country and met carers in Northern Ireland, Wales, Scotland and throughout England. Their accounts of what it meant to be a carer moved me greatly and made me more determined than ever. My authority in tackling the issue came from my academic background. I had also met many carers before, not least through the fledgling carers' movement in Croydon. But my human understanding and, yes, my passion came mainly from the campaign and meeting those magnificent, responsible citizens, some of them almost ground down by their duties, but motivated by their love for those they cared for.

The normal Parliamentary procedure would be for the Bill to go before a Standing Committee for detailed, often line-by-line, scrutiny. But the Committee system for Private Members' Bills was choc-a-bloc and there was a real danger that we would not get it through in time to make progress in the House of Lords. Luck, again, played its part. The Leader of the House of Commons, Tony Newton, was a good friend of the carers' movement and a Tory MP with a strong interest in social policy. Following discussions, he generously (given the time pressures in the Commons), agreed to allocate most of a Friday morning to holding the Committee Stage of the Carers Bill in the Commons chamber itself. This meant that proceedings became a 'Committee of the Whole House' and this impressive event took place on 21st April. Consulting *Hansard*, I see that proceedings got underway at 9.37am and that I spoke for the last time at 1.36pm.

In the weeks preparing for the line-by-line scrutiny that can be expected during the Committee Stage, I had been (together with colleagues from CNA) in detailed discussions with Department of Health officials and lawyers. Until then we had only a draft Bill and we now needed to make sure that its legal underpinning was right. This is something that I later became used to as a Minister, but as a backbencher it was very much a learning game. In Committee, we proceeded through the Bill with proposed amendments in a very detailed way with several backbenchers on both sides contributing. But I also wanted to inject the human dimension, regarding the very purpose of the Bill, into debate. So I quoted examples of what carers in my own borough of Croydon had told me:

*The thing that makes me so angry is that no-one ever asks. No doctor ever says 'do you need help? Have you had any sleep?'*

*Home help service [was] taken away when I got married. My husband also has a disability [but] it was assumed that he would take on the role of home help…We used to have a district nurse for help with a bath – that stopped when I got married. The point is that no consideration is taken about my husband's disabilities.*

*I have had home care withdrawn because my mother and father are regarded as providing sufficient care – my 78-year-old mother is in the early stages of senile dementia and my 80-year-old father has Parkinson's Disease – I now have to rely on friends for help.*

I also highlighted the needs of young carers that we had battled hard to have included in the Bill, telling the story of a boy called Richard:

> *Richard [is] a 12-year-old boy who looks after his mother who has rheumatoid arthritis. His father left the family two years ago, so Richard is the major carer. Before he goes to school, he helps his mother to dress, combs her hair and makes her bed. Some days, he goes home and gets his mother's lunch but he tells his school friends that he is going home to feed the dog in case they laugh at him. When he comes home in the evening, he does the vacuuming, tidies the kitchen and prepares the tea. He then helps his mother have a bath. He often does not manage to finish his homework, which means that he gets into trouble at school. Twice a week, the local authority provides domiciliary care, but some days the woman cannot come, which means extra work for Richard.*

After successfully completing its Committee, Report and Third Reading stages in the Commons, my Bill passed to the House of Lords, where Lord (Denis) Carter skilfully introduced it at Second Reading. Lord Carter had been responsible from the opposition front bench for dealing with the 1990 NHS and Community Care Act; he also had direct experience of caring for a disabled son. As he observed:

> *...our experience then forcibly brought home the situation and the problems of that great army of carers who are often alone and do not receive the help that they should. This Bill will start to put that situation right.* [36]

Lord Carter and other Lords who participated in the debate made it clear that they had no wish to amend the legislation in order that it could pass as quickly as possible into law. Remarkably, the Bill completed its Second Reading in just over an hour.

*A new law – and its aftermath*

After the Carers (Recognition and Services) Act received Royal Assent, the Department of Health issued both policy and practice guidance. The former noted that: "…the effects of the Act will be gradual." Because some local authorities were already offering carers an assessment, the guidance also insisted that: "…the legislation in effect enshrines good practice into statute."[37] It advised that the focus of an assessment "should be on the carer's ability to care and to continue caring" (paragraph 21), and importantly that:

> *It should not automatically assume a willingness by the carer to continue caring, or to continue providing the same level of support.*

The resource implications of the Act were not readily recognised by the Government, and no additional resources were allocated to support its implementation. Nevertheless, a study undertaken for Carers National Association in 1997 examining the impact of the Act found many positive features, including cultural change among local authorities and "a new baseline of rights, with additional recognition and support."[38]

With their needs formally recognised by the 1995 Act, carers gained a toehold in the policy process. Subsequent developments in social care then showed an even greater awareness of carer issues. For example, four years later, under a Labour government, a National Carers' Strategy was introduced for the first time. This had three major elements: information, support, and care. It also addressed a wide range of public policy, including provisions to recognise the responsibilities of carers in employment. A special grant was introduced to help carers to take a break.

I am very proud of the Carers Act 1995, but I have never exaggerated its significance. It was a modest first step, recognising the importance of carers and putting their right to have their own needs assessed on statutory footing. It did not demand that services then flowed and I would never have persuaded the then Government to agree to that. What the Act did do, principally, was to boost morale in carers' organisations and among individual carers themselves[39].

# 10.

# *The Front Bench*

I can always recall in fine detail when I was appointed to ministerial office and this includes becoming a Shadow Minister. I had been asked by the association for the former pupils of Elizabeth College, the 'Old Elizabethans', to be the guest speaker at their London dinner. This was the first time I had attended such a dinner. I had put on my dinner jacket and was struggling with cuff links when the phone rang. It was Tony Blair's office and he was soon on the phone. He wanted me to become one of the Social Security Shadow Ministers. I was relieved, because there was a story out there that he wanted all potential ministers to go through the Whips' Office first. I mentioned this to him and he said words to the effect of: "Yes, but there are exceptions". I was struck by the irony (I hope not hypocrisy) of going off in my dinner jacket to speak to old boys from my public school when I had just secured a Labour Shadow Ministerial role.

Donald Dewar, a wonderful man, was the Shadow Social Security Secretary, and I still recall with a smile our shadow team meetings. These did not usually last long. Keith Bradley, the MP for Manchester Withington, steered us competently through forthcoming Commons business. Clearly things got more complex in the House of Lords because Baroness Patricia Hollis would take much longer, describing to us what was happening in the Upper House and her discussions "on Privy Council terms" with various Tory Ministers. Donald, himself, would guide us delightfully through the proceedings. I remember him regaling us one morning with his version of Ann Widdecombe's very public, conversion to Roman Catholicism, at Westminster Cathedral. He was in fits and I can only imagine that something in his Presbyterian background in Scotland made this such a wonderful occasion for him. That morning no other substantive business was done.

## The 1997 General Election

After the overall disappointment of the 1992 General Election when, despite my own victory, the Tories won again under the leadership of John Major, Labour hopes were sky high for the forthcoming 1997 campaign. John Major's government had witnessed one disaster after another and he faced strong internal dissent from his party's Euro-sceptic right-wingers. Indeed, in desperation, John Major resigned the leadership of the Tory Party in 1995 in order to fight off his opponents. He succeeded, but such a desperate ploy further undermined the credibility of someone who was, fundamentally, a decent man. The deteriorating state of the British economy – not least the 'Black Wednesday' financial crisis (when the Chancellor of the Exchequer, Norman Lamont was forced to remove the pound from the European Exchange Rate Mechanism) – became ingrained in the public mind with Tory failure. The Labour Leader, Tony Blair, was on the crest of a wave, but doing his best to damp down over-extravagant expectations.

In Croydon North we had a wonderful campaign. With large numbers of activists to support us you could tell every day that more and more of the public were moving Labour's way. Our campaign was buoyed by visits from, among others, Tony and Cherie Blair, the Deputy Leader, John Prescott in his battle bus and Peter Mandelson.

My hard-working election organiser was Angela Wilkins. She and I and dozens of others found ourselves working at full tilt. The relationship between organiser and Parliamentary candidate can be a tense one. So, Angela and I challenged each other as to who would lose their temper first. All went well on this front until the final morning of the campaign when I arrived at my office in Thornton Heath High Street to find 20 or more plastic sacks full of rubbish all along the front of the office. This was so completely the wrong image to project on election day that I lost my temper, storming into the office with words to the effect of: "Are we trying to recreate the winter of discontent?" Not only did I lose the challenge with Angela, but I also promptly learned that she and her team of volunteers had stayed up half the night clearing up the office, which inevitably after a four-week campaign was a mess. They had returned the office to a pristine state, anticipating that the black bags would be collected first thing in the morning by the council – which they should have been.

Election days are long, but pass like a whirlwind as the work progresses of encouraging supporters, getting out the vote and calling in on polling stations to see how the turnout looks. There was no real let-up all day and it seemed that 10pm was soon approaching and the close of poll. I then made a mad dash for home to shower and change and eat a small snack. Then on to the count, being held on this occasion in Croydon's Fairfield Halls. It was soon clear from seeing how the counted votes stacked up that we were doing extremely well. But it was only when the result was about to be announced that I came to know the size of my majority. Normally, one would be tipped off a few minutes in advance of the declaration and get the full details. But in 1997 it was only as I peered down at the paper in the hands of the Chief Returning Officer that I realised the extent of my victory. I had won by more than 18,000 votes. This, on slightly different boundaries, was compared to my majority of just 1,400 in 1992. Our supporters were wild with excitement. It was by any measure a tremendous result.

*1997 General Election Result, Croydon North*

| Party | Candidate | Votes | % | +/-% |
|---|---|---|---|---|
| Labour | Malcolm WICKS | 32,672 | 62.2 | n/a |
| Conservative | Ian MARTIN | 14,274 | 27.2 | n/a |
| Liberal Democrat | Martin MORRIS | 4,066 | 7.7 | n/a |
| Referendum Party | R BILLIS | 1,155 | 2.2 | n/a |
| UKIP | J FEISENBERGER | 396 | 0.8 | n/a |
| | **Majority** | 18,398 | | |
| | **Turnout** | | 68.2 | |

*On not becoming a Minister*

Labour's landslide victory became clear and Tony Blair made his memorable daybreak speech at The Royal Festival Hall ("A new dawn has broken, has it not?"). But after he had visited Buckingham Palace and famously walked into 10 Downing Street, cheered by jubilant supporters, our new Prime Minister had to settle down to the task of forming his Government. Having been a Shadow Social Security Minister under Donald Dewar, Chris Smith and then Harriet Harman, I had every right to believe that I was about to be appointed a Parliamentary Under-Secretary at the Department for Social Security. A PM first appoints his Cabinet and a day or two later focuses on the more junior ranks. I waited nervously for the call from 10 Downing Street, but it never came. Eventually the full list of Ministerial appointments was published and I was all too obviously not included. No one ever phoned me to explain that this time there would be no place for me; and that, I suppose, is typical of the general chaos surrounding Ministerial appointments and, later, reshuffles. Certainly, the Labour Party is not at its best when it comes to managing HR!

Two explanations were possible. One, which I rather discounted, though it has been suggested to me by one or two colleagues, was that my own approach to social security with its Titmuss–inspired emphasis on universal benefits (see Chapter 5), was out of line with the thinking of Gordon Brown, the new Chancellor of the Exchequer, and his team. I certainly once had an exchange of views with Gordon's adviser, Ed Balls[40], where I discovered, somewhat to my surprise, that he was no friend of universal Child Benefit and something of a means tester. However, I never gave this conspiracy theory any credence. Rather, I think the explanation was simple. Tony Blair appointed Frank Field as Minister of State for Welfare Reform and, as Frank had not been a member of the shadow team, this meant that there was one less place for those of us who had been Shadow Ministers. I had simply lost out, but it would have been nice if someone had phoned me to explain.

I found myself in a curious position. Some days later Harriet Harman, the new Secretary of State for Social Security, telephoned me and said that she could not understand why I was not there in her Department as a Minister. I replied, perhaps somewhat tartly, that I could not understand it either. She proposed that I should become Chairman of the Commons Social Security Committee and rather guaranteed me the appointment. This was, of course, back in the bad old days when chairmanships of select committees were determined through the Whips' Office with a heavy steer from Cabinet Ministers. I am glad to say that extension of executive patronage has gone and it is MPs themselves who determine who should chair our backbench committees. However, even under the old system the promise made to me was never fulfilled. A day or two later a senior Whip approached me and said that they wished me to become the "senior member" of the select committee. I queried this: "Do you mean Chairman?" The Whip looked embarrassed and explained that it had been agreed that a Liberal Democrat should chair one select committee and, of course, that turned out to be social security.

This was yet another setback because, while I wished to become a Minister, I could see that a period chairing a select committee would have been fulfilling. Fortunately things promptly got better – not least because Archy Kirkwood, the then MP for Roxburgh and Berwickshire was the Liberal Democrat choice for Chair. I already had a great deal of respect for him and he was soon on the phone. He insisted that the committee would only work if he and I worked closely together, and this is just what we did for the next year or so. However, after a year that included a memorable and educational visit to the USA (when we visited Wisconsin to investigate their novel, part-positive, part-draconian, approach to welfare) I was unexpectedly asked to become Chairman of the Education Select Committee instead. Again, to be blunt, this was down to patronage. The then Secretary of State for Education, David Blunkett, offered me the position, which was duly agreed through 'the usual channels'. This was to the initial irritation of some of the Labour MPs that were already on the select committee who must have seen me as something of an interloper.

We undertook a number of enquiries, including one into highly able or 'gifted' children. But our most important enquiry, and certainly the most controversial, was into the schools' inspection service, Ofsted. Ofsted's then Chief Inspector was Chris Woodhead. At one stage, early in his career, he had been seen as an education progressive, but now his reputation was that of someone who had become a conservative in his approach to standards and tradition. He enjoyed strong support at 10 Downing Street but, I would say there was less enthusiasm for his approach from David Blunkett. As part of the Ofsted enquiry, I suggested to my fellow committee members that we should, as individuals, arrange to observe Ofsted's inspectors in action, at both primary and secondary school levels. I certainly found the experience of being with them for a day, and the opportunity to talk to inspectors, heads and teachers very illuminating.

There was, however, one classroom I visited where a tendency towards over-inspection might have been apparent. Alongside the actual Ofsted inspector, one of Her Majesty's Inspectors of School was also present. So in the classroom, we had the strange spectacle of a schools inspector observing the classroom performance of what turned out to be a very competent teacher, while, in turn, being observed by an HM Inspector. Meanwhile, sitting at the back of the class, was the Chairman of the House of Commons Select Committee on Education observing the whole process. I have to say that the teacher conducted a very good class and, talking to her later, I was impressed how unfazed she was by this rather extraordinary exercise in monitoring.

## On becoming a Minister

I had rather assumed that I would be staying as Chair of the Education Select Committee for some years, which was the normal situation. But less than a year later, in July 1999, I received − at last − the call from 10 Downing Street telling me that the Prime Minister would like to see me. It was still a period of New Labour enthusiasm and the atmosphere around the Party and Government was extremely positive. I walked up Downing Street as coolly as possible in the most exciting of circumstances. My son, Roger, who worked at the BBC, saw my progress towards No 10 and rang my wife to suggest she turn on the

TV. After a while I was ushered into Tony Blair's office where he appointed me Parliamentary Under-Secretary of State in the Department for Education and Employment (DfEE), working for David Blunkett. There was some initial confusion about my role. Tony thought that I might become the junior schools minister, taking the place of Charles Clarke who was moving on to the Home Office. But he also said that David might have other ideas. In fact I became the Minister for Lifelong Learning.

On becoming a Minister, as I have written elsewhere (see 'What Ministers Do' in Part 2), your life is transformed. You are suddenly surrounded by a formidable support system. A ministerial car materialises. I found myself whisked off to the DfEE headquarters in Great Smith Street; there to be met by my new Private Secretary who introduced me to the rest of the private office. A private office for someone of my rank consisted, typically of four – normally young – officials. Soon, thereafter, I was introduced to the Department's Permanent Secretary, the very talented Michael Bichard, and to the senior civil servant with responsibility for the main areas I would be dealing with. A Ministerial meeting called by David Blunkett then took place and so, very quickly, I was in harness.

The DfEE, was a very large department covering not only the entirety of education, from nurseries to universities, but also employment. It therefore handled a number of key initiatives by the Labour Government, including *Sure Start* for the under-5s and the *New Deal for Youth* to tackle unemployment. I joined a very talented team of ministers. There was David Blunkett, of course, as Secretary of State, but also Andrew Smith, the Employment Minister, Tessa Blackstone (Universities), Estelle Morris (School Standards), Jacqui Smith (junior School Standards Minister), Tessa Jowell (Employment, Welfare to Work and Equal Opportunities), Margaret Hodge (Employment and Equal Opportunities) and Michael Wills (Information Technology in Schools). David Blunkett was, without doubt, the most driven and hard-working Secretary of State I ever worked with. And, of course, he had to work far harder than any other politician because of his lack of sight. His staff would put much of the material he needed to read on to tape, while many of his papers needed to be transcribed into Braille. Moreover, David would put work onto tape himself. I suspect that all of this added many hours to his working week.

Although David took a great deal of interest in all aspects of the Department it was schools that had to command most of his attention on the education side of his responsibilities. The Labour Government was committed to raising standards, very often in the teeth of opposition from the education establishment, including the teachers' unions. Too many schools were failing their pupils; too many others were simply coasting along. I once experienced the vehemence of the teaching profession at a conference in Kent. The head of a local primary school was metaphorically spitting blood at me and proclaimed: "How dare ministers tell us how to teach when we have the experience, when we are the experts?" I did my best to tell him that too many children were leaving primary school without the required levels of literacy or numeracy, so making it more difficult for them to progress at secondary school. So David and his schools team had to impose 'literacy hours' in schools and set times for numeracy, both of which were regarded as a great interference. Yet for several years standards in schools increased. There were also issues about the structure of the schools system and the development of the 'Academy' idea[41]. Andrew Adonis, then a Downing Street special adviser on education, was a frequent presence in the Department.

My own portfolio, lifelong learning, was one close to David Blunkett's heart; not least, I suspect, given his own history and background. In simple terms, while there was a well-understood route to university in Britain, the alternative routes for the majority of people who did not go to university were either less clear (and certainly less well-funded) or non-existent. There existed a fundamental cultural problem; namely that, for most people, education and learning somehow simply ended when they left school. And yet, given the fast-

Malcolm with his father, Arthur

A keen footballer,
until the knee injury!

With his elder brother Keith,
in the Isle of Wight

Carrying the banner, Aldermaston March, 1963

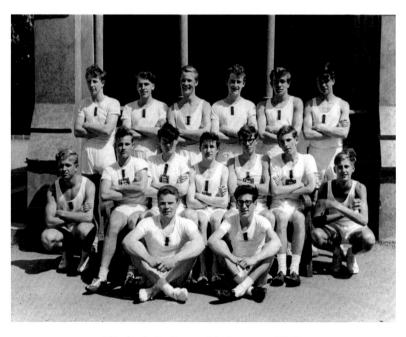

Elizabeth College athletics team, 1964.
Backrow, second right

Malcolm and Maggie's wedding,
Alderney, Channel Islands, 1968

Chairman of the Greater London Council, Arthur Wicks, with
Malcolm and Professor David Donnison, 1973

With his mother Daisy, and Keith, 1973

Sanderstead ward by-election with Michael Foot, 1984

Croydon South delegate, Labour Party Conference, Blackpool, 1986

Malcolm's first general election victory announced by Mayor Jim
Walker, Croydon North West, 1992

Bosnia with Kate Hoey and Calum MacDonald, 1993

With great friend Tony Hall,
celebrating the England cricket team winning at Lord's

Labour wins Croydon Council, 1994

The Thornton Heath Festival

South Norwood Safer Neighbourhood Team

On the Front Bench

Promoting science with 'Wallace & Gromit'

Introduction of the Pension Credit Scheme with actress Elizabeth
Dawn and Andrew Smith, DWP Secretary of State, 2003

Opening the Artfield Fell wind
farm, Scotland, 2005

An off-shore oil rig in the
North Sea

En route to the Elgin Franklin oil rigs from Aberdeen, 2005

Astronauts at NASA, 2006

Drilling an ice core with Lord Ronald Oxburgh, in Rothera, with the
British Antarctic Survey, 2007

On holiday in Alderney with Maggie

With their children, Roger, Caroline and Sarah
at Sarah's wedding, 2006

Kensington Avenue Primary School

Giving a tour of the House of Commons
to the Harris Academy debating team

Franco British Summit with Jacques Chirac,
at the Élysée Palace, 2006

Public meeting on the NHS with John Healey MP
and Croydon Councillor Tony Newman

Honorary Doctorate, Brunel University, 2009

Whitgift Almshouses, Croydon

The Grandchildren,
from the top,
Matthew, Cameron,
Anna,
Rebecca, Sophie,
Miriam and Enrico

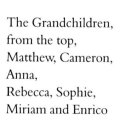

changing nature of the global economy, with declining employment in manufacturing industry and fewer jobs that young people could simply walk into at 16, skills and education were becoming more important. I paint the picture somewhat darkly, because apprenticeships still existed and many employees improved their skills, either in the workplace, or via evening classes. Nevertheless, too little of this kind of work-related learning was taking place.

We needed, especially, to boost the role and quality of further education (FE) colleges, all too often referred to as a 'Cinderella' service. In November 1999, I had the agreeable task of announcing the extra funding that was required. David Blunkett should have been making the announcement to the Association of Colleges' conference in Harrogate, but, as luck would have it, the Queen's Speech debate on 23 November was on education and employment. This meant that David had to make the 'wind-up' speech. I was, therefore, deputed to announce a record 10 per cent increase in funding for further education, which was the largest ever in history. During my time as a DfEE Minister I visited a large number of FE colleges and witnessed some very good work in teaching. My only quibble was that more or less every college seemed to be teaching 'hair and beauty'. I found myself wondering how many hair salons and beauty parlours the UK actually needed – and whether working in such places would really help young people to develop worthwhile careers at good wages.

## Ho, Ho, Ho Chi Minh!

Life at the DfEE was made more pleasant by the fact that Margaret Hodge, who became a Minister of State, was a fine organiser of social occasions. One evening she invited the whole Ministerial Team to her house in North London for dinner. It was a convivial occasion. Tessa Blackstone, another Minister of State, had just returned from a visit to Vietnam and presented us all with busts of the late communist leader, Ho Chi Minh. Our thoughts immediately went back to the Vietnam War and it became clear that several of us had taken part in protest marches during that period. An old slogan was remembered and suddenly there was the incongruous sight of a number of Tony Blair's New Labour Ministers chanting: "Ho, Ho, Ho Chi Minh. You're the man that's going to win!"

One of my other major responsibilities, and certainly one of the most challenging and rewarding, was the development of the *Connexions* youth support service[42]. When I got to the DfEE I discovered quickly that although planning was already in progress, not much work had actually been done. In fact I had a somewhat surreal meeting with an official who had some responsibility for *Connexions* but also, in an honorary capacity, looked after the DfEE gym. I expressed some interest in going to the gym (an interest that was not subsequently pursued) and came away from our meeting knowing, regrettably, far more about the gym facilities than about *Connexions*. Nevertheless, a strong team was soon assembled to make a reality of the new service, headed by the formidable Anne Weinstock[43] who was ably supported by Claire Tyler[44].

*Connexions* was a response to the inadequacies of the existing schools careers service but also, more critically, to a realisation that too many children needed to be given a second or third chance to improve their education and skills. As part of our quest to boost opportunities (and not just for those destined for university) we recognised that schools, for too many children, were almost irrelevant. Given a setback – teenage pregnancy, a brush with the law or an involvement with drugs, for example – their education was virtually over without anyone there to pick up the pieces. Of course, many agencies might engage with a young person and their family (perhaps the police, social services, probation, and a voluntary organisation or two) but there were no mechanisms for focusing these services on the young person in a co-ordinated way.

As a Minister, I recognised that getting this right was no easy matter. Earlier in my career I had studied the 1968 Seebohm Report, calling for the reorganisation of social services, and I knew about the difficulties of bringing about co-ordination in practice. I was also aware of other brave attempts to bring comprehensive, multi-agency strategies into being, such as the *Joint Approach to Social Policy* pioneered in the 1970s by the then Central Policy Review Staff. This meant that I relished the opportunity to see if we could make *Connexions* work.

---

### A walkout averted

One of the key roles for a Minister is to get around the country, to make speeches and to meet up with some of the key institutions in the field. Education in general, and lifelong learning in particular, were never short of such encounters. On one such occasion the National Association of Teachers of Further and Higher Education [NATFHE] were meeting at Blackpool for their annual conference and I was the main guest speaker. On arriving in Blackpool I was warned that the more militant delegates were planning to walk out from the conference hall during my speech. I decided to make things difficult for them. At the start of my speech I outlined its contents and three or four subjects I wanted to cover. I then added that I hoped this outline would make the planning of the protest walkout easier. Many of the delegates laughed; the militants looked sullen. No one walked out.

---

# 11.

# Pensions, Energy and Science

[In the June 2001 General Election, MW was re-elected as MP for Croydon North with a majority of 16,858 which, on a lower turnout than in 1997, represented a further swing towards Labour.

*2001 General Election Result, Croydon North*

| Party | Candidate | Votes | % | +/-% |
|---|---|---|---|---|
| Labour | Malcolm WICKS | 26,610 | 63.5 | +1.4 |
| Conservative | Simon ALLISON | 9,752 | 23.3 | -3.9 |
| Liberal Democrat | Sandra LAWMAN | 4,375 | 10.4 | +2.7 |
| UKIP | Alan SMITH | 606 | 1.4 | +0.7 |
| Socialist Alliance | Don MADGWICK | 539 | 1.3 | N/A |
| | **Majority** | 16,858 | | |
| | **Turnout** | | 53.2 | |

In the Government re-shuffle that followed the election he was made Parliamentary Under-Secretary at the Department for Work and Pensions (DWP) and, in 2003, was promoted to become Minister of State for Pensions.]

## *The National Pensioners' Convention (and other demos)*

Just days after my appointment as Minister of State for Pensions in July 2003, the National Pensioners' Convention was due to hold its annual conference and rally in Blackpool. Hundreds gathered for this event and it was well known that it provided an opportunity for delegates to vent their anger at the hapless minister of the day. This quaint tradition of shouting, heckling and generally trying to deny the Minister a hearing has since spread to be a feature of conferences held by, among others, the police, nurses and teachers. Since I was so new in the job, my civil servants argued against my attending. But it was a movement that I knew well and its President, the retired trade union leader Rodney Bickerstaffe, was a friend. I thought it would be cowardly to refuse and, to be honest, I rather relished the challenge.

Rodney did his best to calm things down, imploring delegates to give the Minister a fair hearing, not least because I was extraordinarily new to office. In fact they did give me a very fair hearing which must have lasted all of 90 seconds. Then the shouting and the catcalls started, becoming louder and louder. However, I managed to get through my speech. I had to get back to London so, having been thanked by Rodney, I started to leave. With impressive speed, a delegate in his late 70s ran after me and shouted: "You're as twisted as a corkscrew, Mr Wicks!" All in all I thought it had gone rather well.

A little later during my pensions tenure, when I embarked on a short tour in the South West of England, there was a particular individual in Devon who led a somewhat militant pensioners' group that we knew we would run into sooner or later. I was due to speak at a conference and as our car drove in we saw a rather impressive demonstration ready to receive us. The gentleman in question was dressed as an old-fashioned funeral director in a long black coat and black top hat. A coffin was in full view. The main banner proclaimed: "We come to bury Malcolm Wicks, not to praise him." I recognised the fine Shakespearean reference and thought it a cut above a mere "twisted corkscrew".

To add to the sense of occasion, the regional TV stations had sent camera crews and reporters. But what to do? It would be stupid to sweep past them in the car, even though I was due to speak in the next two minutes at the conference. I decided to get out and approach the demonstration on the reasonable grounds that it was unlikely this act of foolhardiness would result in me ending up in the coffin. I think the demonstrators respected the fact that I spoke to them for a while, with cameras pointing at me. There was some very good-natured heckling and then it was over. The demonstration was a good one, it got them ample TV coverage and I made my way, unscathed, to speak at the conference.

## Protecting pensions

One big challenge that came to the fore during my time at the DWP was the scandal in some businesses whereby employees, and existing occupational pensioners, were at risk of losing a substantial proportion of their final salary pensions if the company went bust. The employees and former employees of several companies suffered this fate. The credit for putting some energy and policy-making motion into this problem went to Ian McCartney, then MP for Makerfield and my predecessor as Pensions Minister. This was not an easy, and certainly not an inexpensive, problem to solve. Some even questioned whether the state had any real obligation here. However, like Ian, I was convinced that it did. And I was even more convinced after I had met some of the workers who were directly affected. These were hard-working men and women – often skilled workers operating in tough conditions – who had joined their company pensions scheme when they were as young as 15 or 16. Suddenly, as their company ran into difficulties, they could see the income they had saved, and looked forward to in retirement, diminishing.

But it was difficult territory. No one knew how many company schemes might be affected in the future. And what should be done about a scheme where the crisis had already occurred? There was a great deal of caution concerning the right response and, as ever, reluctance on the part of the Treasury to commit itself. Fortunately, pressure from the affected workers and from MPs helped us to move forward. In what became the Pensions Act of 2004 we were not only able to legislate for a Pension Protection Fund, but also for a supplementary Financial Assistance Scheme (FAS) to help those who had already lost their pensions. We had to legislate in haste; something that all reasonable people – especially Parliamentarians, lawyers, experts and Parliamentary Counsel – warn against. However these were not reasonable times and it was grossly unreasonable and unjust that people were losing their pensions. We needed to act quickly.

The Pensions Bill we introduced was hardly, at first, the finished article. At its Committee Stage we were still re-writing the legislation as we went along. It fell to me to move hundreds and hundreds of government amendments; almost a thousand, I think. The outcome was, however, an excellent one. By 2005, the Pension Protection Fund (PPF) was up and running, paid for by a levy on existing final salary company pension schemes. It guaranteed workers 90 per cent of their pension rights up to a generous cap, and 100 per cent for those who had already retired from the company. By July 2012, more than 65,600 people were being helped by the PPF and a further 25,597 by the FAS. The scheme runs smoothly and (a good sign) is seldom discussed. I take some satisfaction from the action we took and the significant number of people that we succeeded in helping.

[In the May 2005 General Election, the voters of Croydon North re-elected Malcolm Wicks.

*2005 General Election Result, Croydon North*

| Party | Candidate | Votes | % | +/-% |
|---|---|---|---|---|
| Labour | Malcolm WICKS | 23,555 | 53.7 | –9.8 |
| Conservative | Tariq AHMAD | 9,667 | 22.0 | –1.3 |
| Liberal Democrat | Adrian GEE-TURNER | 7,590 | 17.3 | +6.8 |
| Green Party | Shasha KHAN | 1,248 | 2.8 | N/A |
| UKIP | Henry PEARCE | 770 | 1.8 | +0.4 |
| Croydon Pensions Alliance | Peter GIBSON | 394 | 0.9 | N/A |
| Veritas | Winston MCKENZIE | 324 | 0.7 | N/A |
| Independent | Farhan RASHEED | 197 | 0.4 | N/A |
| People's Choice | Michelle CHAMBERS | 132 | 0.3 | N/A |
| | **Majority** | 13,888 | | |
| | **Turnout** | | 52.3 | |

In the country as a whole, Labour, led by Tony Blair, was returned to power for an historic third consecutive term in office.]

## *Reshuffled (again)*

Following a General Election, or when the summer recess approaches, rumours start to circulate about the likely consequences of an imminent Ministerial reshuffle. Names are mentioned in the press and potential winners and losers are speculated upon. It is a nervous time for all concerned. When the reshuffle gets underway Cabinet Ministers are the first to be selected or deselected. Only then does the Prime Minister, perhaps the next day, attend to the middle and junior ranks. During my nine years as a Minister, I went through this nervous experience, when my own position was directly affected, some seven times.

The key question on reshuffle day is what to do with yourself. It would not be appropriate to assume that you are staying on in the same Ministerial role, so you keep well away from the Department. On the other hand, you want to be around Westminster somewhere to receive a call from 10 Downing Street, even if it's only to say that you have been dismissed. It is an immensely frustrating time. So, having served as Pensions Minister for two years up to 2005 – a role I had enjoyed immensely – I found myself on reshuffle day, wandering somewhat aimlessly around St James's Park, rather late in the afternoon, wondering why on earth my mobile phone hadn't yet rung.

Finally the call came: "Are you available to speak to the Prime Minister?" There can only be one answer to that question. "Malcolm, I want you to become Energy Minister." As the Prime Minister said this I remember having some feeling of the immense complexity of his task with so many portfolios to fill, and lists of names all around him. But having waited all day for the call I found myself saying: "Thank you, but at DWP at least I knew something of the subject, but

I can't pretend to be an expert in energy policy". Tony Blair simply replied that: "A little humility on these occasions is a good thing." And that's how you become Energy Minister.

But it was a new subject for me. The only area where I had any real knowledge and expertise related to my past research on hypothermia and the book I had subsequently written (see Chapter 4).

[As Minister of State for Energy in the Department of Trade and Industry (DTI), MW held responsibility for energy issues, sustainability and the environment. The portfolio also included corporate social responsibility and fuel poverty. He led the energy review published in 2006, so playing a key role on the subject of nuclear energy. He based a number of reflections on incidents from this period in his Ministerial career in his paper for the *Political Quarterly* 'What Ministers Do'. This is reproduced in Part 2. However, the relevant passage in his memoirs was left incomplete at his death, apart from the following anecdote:]

### Dentistry and diplomacy in Vilnius

One morning, while Energy Minister, I travelled with my team to Vilnius, the capital of Lithuania. The Lithuanians were holding a regional summit and it was considered important that the UK attended and made its contribution. Unfortunately, the day before, I chipped a tooth – though the problem was not so much the tooth itself but the fact that it was rubbing against the inside of my mouth. There was no time to deal with it in London, so at the airport I bought some chewing gum and fixed a blob on the offending tooth. I had hoped this home remedy would see me through the day, but it lasted for about five minutes.

This was hardly a medical emergency but I told my Private

Secretary about the problem. We arrived at the conference centre in Vilnius and I took the UK seat. Soon, the British Ambassador was at my side ready to apply his diplomatic skills to my dental problem. He explained that there were excellent dentists in Lithuania and that they could quietly and discreetly whisk me away to see one that the embassy knew. I would hardly be gone half an hour and the problem would be solved there and then. Things were fixed so that I could give my speech early, the Ambassador could take over the UK seat and I could be off for my discreet dental appointment.

Things turned out somewhat differently. No one seemed to think that I could get in a car and go to the dentist on my own. My Private Secretary insisted on coming (a good PS never lets the minister out of sight!), but then an interpreter appeared 'just in case'. The protocol officer who had been assigned to me by the Lithuanian Government also joined the party – why, I don't know, but presumably in case my opening my mouth as wide as possible created a diplomatic incident.

A small convoy of vehicles then headed off, led by a police car sounding its siren. We also acquired motorcycle outriders and, much to my embarrassment, traffic was stopped at roundabouts so that the British chipped tooth repair would not be delayed.

The dentist was excellent and she remedied things quickly and professionally. But by the time the whole shebang had been repeated on the return journey, all hope of secrecy and discretion had evaporated. The first delegate I saw was the head of the American delegation: "Tooth OK now, Malcolm?" he wryly enquired.

## Science Minister

I had been Energy Minister for 18 months when my responsibilities changed again, initially in bizarre circumstances. Some officials and I were travelling back on Eurostar, from Brussels, after a long day in the conference room. Anxious to get home I must have left my mobile phone on the train. Getting into the back of the Ministerial car, my driver's phone rang and it was 10 Downing Street wanting to talk to me. "You left your phone on Eurostar", said the operator.

I was naturally impressed that they knew this, and even more amazed that they were phoning to tell me, notwithstanding the formidable reputation that the No 10 Downing Street telephone staff enjoy for always finding their man or woman. I thanked the operator and was about to put the phone down when she said: "No, hold on. The Prime Minister wishes to talk to you". Tony Blair explained that David Sainsbury[45] was stepping down as Science Minister at DTI and that he wished me to take his place. Taken aback, I said to Tony that this would come as a big surprise to my science teachers. He laughed and wished me good luck[46].

Being appointed Science Minister came as an enormous surprise to me and, I suppose at the time, something of a disappointment. I was totally engaged in the Energy portfolio and wanted to continue with that work. David Sainsbury had been Science Minister since 1998 and had done a tremendous job, including securing funds that enabled the Government's science budget to double in size. The reality for his successor was that it wasn't about to double in size again.

My main concern as Science Minister was to communicate to a wider public that science and the innovations that flow from it were essential to the so-called 'knowledge economy' that the UK needed to become. With a declining proportion of businesses and jobs in traditional sectors, the UK needed to live by its wits. Building a strong science base was critical. That is why we put a Technology Strategy Board in place to push innovation and focus resources in some critical areas. I also sought to develop a more general narrative about science and society to convince the public that science spending was well worthwhile, and to demonstrate how it related in practical terms to many different aspects of British life.

## *Satellites, dementia and the* Daily Mirror

One of my keen interests during my brief period as Science Minister was satellite technology. I discovered that, while the UK was not in the business of sending astronauts into space, we were very good at the development of very small satellites and that the University of Surrey was a centre of excellence.

When the Commons Science Committee undertook an enquiry into satellites I was called before them. We discussed various applications of satellite technology, including the way they could help farmers monitor food production and how they could help the shipping industry to find the best possible route. Then, some way into the discussion, I argued that satellites might also prove helpful when it came to the rapidly emerging problem of dementia and Alzheimer's Disease:

> *"I just wonder myself, coming from a social science and social policy background, whether we do not need to develop another strand of our thinking to see whether some of the issues we face in terms of our society and social policy could not be helped by the development of suitable satellite technology and monitoring. I am thinking of the issue, for example, of the care of an increasingly elderly and frail population where many, many families and communities are worried about what is happening to their 80 or 90-year-old person who may have Alzheimer's or something. Surely if we are able to do traffic monitoring we should be able, in the best sense, to do people monitoring where there are concerns. I think we could bring some technologies together there, with all the sensitivities we need to apply of course to avoid a Big Brother approach, there could be some useful applications in our welfare state which I would quite like to explore."* [Select Committee on Science & Technology, Seventh Report, 2007: *A Space Policy*, HC 66-II Minutes of Evidence, Q599]

I thought this a perfectly sensible idea that deserved exploration, but the *Daily Mirror* pounced on the story. I arrived at work the next morning to be informed that the paper had launched an all-out attack.

> *"Tagging the elderly like criminals has all the horror of a Big Brother nightmare. Tracking senior citizens by satellite and attaching electronic bracelets to their ankles would be a step too far in a supposedly free country. Criminals are monitored because they are a threat to society, supervised to stop them stealing or even killing."*

The *Mirror* went on to argue that *"Science Minister, Malcolm Wicks, should retract his unacceptable proposals or he will deservedly face public derision."*

Of course, I had never likened sufferers from dementia to criminals, nor had I ever advocated attaching electronic bracelets to their ankles. But lies and distortion can be all the way around the world before rationality gets a look in. It even occurred to me that this controversy might prove to be a career-defining moment: I might get sacked! Fortunately, the debate did become more rational after the *Mirror* to their credit, invited the Chief Executive of the Alzheimer's Society, Neil Hunt, to argue the 'yes' case, with the President of the National Pensioners' Convention representing the 'no' corner.

Politicians must develop a thick skin and most of the time my skin was thick enough. Yet this was personally upsetting: I had a strong association with the Alzheimer's Society, Carers UK and Age Concern. A close family member had suffered from Alzheimer's for a very long period and I had witnessed the family's anxieties at first hand. I was therefore grateful that the Alzheimer's Society offered their support with sensible words drawing on their own experience:

*Many people with dementia feel compelled to walk about and there is a high risk of getting lost. For people with dementia and their carers this 'wandering' can be a very real worry. Electronic tagging has the potential to ease these concerns and empower people who have dementia, giving them confidence and independence.*

The controversy provoked an interesting correspondence, particularly letters from carers. One particularly moving one told how an elderly man suffering from Alzheimer's went out for a walk and alarm bells rang for his family when, some hours later, he had not returned. Much later he was found dead on the beach and his wife wanted me to know that perhaps, if the technology I was talking about had been in place, he could have been found much earlier and his life saved[47].

## To the Antarctic

While I cannot claim that my contribution to the development of science was immense, I learned a great deal myself. When Chris Rapley, Director of the British Antarctic Survey (BAS), wrote to me in the first few days of my tenure, he invited me to visit the Antarctic. This, in many respects, ranks as the most memorable visit I have ever made. A small group of us ventured out on a military aircraft from RAF Brize Norton, stopping over for just a couple of hours on Ascension Island. Then it was on to the Falkland Islands for an overnight stay at Government House. I took the opportunity of exploring Port Stanley and studied the war memorial there for those British troops whose lives were lost, retaking the islands after the Argentinian invasion in

1982. The next morning we flew into Rothera where the BAS is based. Then, for three or four memorable days, I was introduced to the range of research being undertaken: marine biology, the study of bird life and, critically, work on climate change.

Although I did not need convincing about the reality of climate change my visit to Antarctica had a profound impact on me – and one that was reinforced when I subsequently met Al Gore, the former American Vice-President and international climate campaigner, in London. These events were not only important for me as Science Minister, but also when I subsequently returned to my role as Energy Minister. Although energy policy involves juggling a number of objectives, I had no doubt that reducing carbon dioxide ($CO_2$) levels was the most important one. That is why I was a firm advocate of energy efficiency, renewable energy and, indeed, nuclear power.

I remember how we spent one night of my Antarctic visit under canvas on a highish point above the Rothera base. There I was introduced to the extraction of ice cores. The ice core that I managed to extract myself was only about a foot or so in length, but the length of some of the ice cores retrieved is considerable and of great scientific importance because they enable us to know about the $CO_2$ levels that existed hundreds of thousands of years ago. They are an important means of monitoring global warming and the British work in this field is of major international significance.

It turned out, however, that I was only to be in post as Science Minister for seven months; not really enough time to get to grips with the subject or to work out what my own contribution could be. Unlike my Ministerial posts at DWP, I could not expect to hit the ground running, drawing on the knowledge I already had of the subject. I needed time to fully understand my new portfolio. And since Gordon Brown, on succeeding Tony Blair in June 2007, promptly asked me to return to the energy portfolio, I never had the time to do that.

[MW continued in government, resuming his work as Minister of State for Energy from June 2007 until October 2008. Some further reflections on climate change and other energy issues can be found in his *Political Quarterly* essay 'What Ministers Do', reproduced in Part 2.]

# 12.

# *Return to the Backbenches*

I have described the worries, frustrations and traumas associated with Ministerial reshuffles. Much of this anxiety is due to the fact that, sooner or later, you know that your Ministerial career will end. The Prime Minister will be calling not to give you a new post or offer you promotion, but to take your job away from you. Enoch Powell may not have been entirely accurate when he said that all political lives, unless cut off in midstream, "end in failure"[48] but his suggestion does have a real ring of truth about it.

By the autumn of 2008 Britain's economic and financial landscape was changing in the wake of a financial crisis whose enormous consequences were beginning to become apparent. Prime Minister Gordon Brown was at full stretch, and it was no surprise that this was to have implications for the Ministerial team. A reshuffle duly took place and I, finally, received a call from 10 Downing Street.

When Gordon came on the phone I, for some reason, felt the need to break the ice: "Gordon, you're having a tough day". I was aware that, following the reshuffle, he would soon be on his way to Paris for a global summit on the banking crisis. "Yes, Malcolm," he replied, "and I need your help on this one". My Ministerial career was about to end. Gordon explained that he needed to appoint some people with real financial experience into Ministerial posts. I said I understood. But he then said that he wished to continue using my expertise and that he hoped that I would agree to become his Special Representative on International Energy Issues, working with a team of officials to produce an authoritative report on energy security.

There had, by then, been a number of 'envoy' posts dished out to sacked Ministers and I am afraid I was rather cynical. Feeling that it was better to end my Ministerial career there and then, rather than take on a role for the sake of it, I remember saying to Gordon: "I do think this 'Envoy to the Rain Forests' stuff is past its sell-by date." But he persevered in a way that I still find remarkable for someone who was under such pressure at that time, and for someone who supposedly had such a brusque manner. He said he had always respected my work, that as a university teacher he had used my books and that he really would like me to take on this new role. I could not simply say 'no' and promised him that I would think about it overnight. I had, after all, a respect for the office of Prime Minister and, indeed, a respect for Gordon himself. The next day I phoned 10 Downing Street and said that I would do it as long as there was adequate support from Whitehall and that I could work with a team of top officials.

## Securing energy supplies

One prime reason for accepting Gordon Brown's offer was my genuine concerns about Britain's energy security. Energy policy involves balancing a number of important objectives, not least climate change. But while I was confident that we were moving in the right direction on climate change, not least because Parliament had legislated for strict $CO_2$ reduction targets, I was less confident that Whitehall and Parliament had grasped the significance of potential energy insecurities. Britain was becoming much more dependent on energy from abroad, some of it from volatile places. I was also conscious that we depended quite heavily on non-British companies for our imports and supply.

One meeting, from my time as Energy Minister, stood out in my mind. During the difficult winter of 2005/06, I had called together the representatives of major energy suppliers to assess the situation. One by one, the company executives gave their reports and sought to assure me that supplies would be adequate that winter (which, indeed, they were).

But it suddenly struck me that many of those present were talking with foreign accents. They came from Germany, France, the USA and different parts of the Middle East. Most of the companies they represented were not British. Many of these executives would, no doubt be working in other countries in a year or two's time. So the question occurred to me: "Where is the British interest here?" I hope this was not mere jingoism on my part, but genuinely reflected a more grounded concern about the security of our energy. Not surprisingly, I recall that during the same winter a very senior British executive of a German company – one of our six key energy suppliers – told me I should always remember that energy supply to Germany was the company's principal concern. German Chancellors had been known to call in the chief executive of his company to remind him where his loyalties should lie. And all this was during a period when the gas interconnector[49] linking the UK to European supplies was failing to deliver enough gas to Britain (despite the high prices being offered) because long-term contracts in Germany meant that our requests for support were being denied.

My work for Gordon Brown as his Special Representative proved fulfilling. We drew on the wisdom of an 'expert group' and visited Oslo, Washington, Brussels and the International Energy Agency in Paris. I was supported by an able team from the Department of Energy and Climate Change, and we worked closely with the Foreign & Commonwealth Office. My report, published in 2009, concluded that there was no immediate crisis, but that the time had come to consider a more active and interventionist role for the state in securing future energy supplies. Alongside intensified action to increase supplies from renewable energy sources and a re-examination of the 'clean' use of coal reserves, I also recommended that the Government aspire beyond 2030 to provide some 35-40 per cent of Britain's electricity from nuclear energy. My Introduction to the report gives a flavour of its overall findings:

*The geopolitics of energy insecurity will be a key theme for the 21st century. Securing Britain's energy supply must therefore be a national priority as we transition to a low carbon economy. We have entered a decade or more of dramatic transition, heralding a century of serious energy uncertainty. We are moving from a position of relative energy independence to one of significant dependence on imports. Gas is critical, given its importance to industry, electricity generation and home heating. In recent years Britain was self-sufficient; today we are net importers of over 25% of our annual demand; and by 2020 this proportion will be considerably higher. Estimates of import dependence by 2020 range from 45% to much higher, 70% or more.*

*There is no crisis. Indeed we are doing many of the things that are important. The build-up of renewables to a target of 15% of all energy by 2020; the decision to facilitate a new generation of civil nuclear plants; and a number of energy efficiency programmes all help to produce a better balance between home-grown energy and imports. I welcome the UK Low Carbon Transition Plan, which sets out in detail how we will achieve the challenging climate change targets we have adopted. It is a major contributor to our future energy security.*

*But there is no room for complacency. As the world comes out of global recession, the global grab for energy will return to something like its pre-recession trajectory, with demand forecast to increase substantially by 2030. Oil and gas prices can be expected to increase, perhaps very significantly. More nations will flex their muscles in the pursuit of energy resources.*

*This presents new challenges. There is no exact science on this, more a question of risk assessment and judgement. But the loss of relative energy self-sufficiency takes place at a time of rapid energy change and challenge. My conclusion is that the era of heavy reliance on companies, competition and liberalisation must be re-assessed. The time for market innocence is over. We must still rely on companies for exploration, delivery and supply, but the state must become more active – interventionist where necessary. This is critical in Europe, when, despite progress, full liberalisation of energy has not been achieved, and when key states are strong players in energy decision-making. Moreover, internationally, independent private-sector oil companies control smaller proportions of global oil and gas reserves, as nation states use national companies to develop these national resources. Many countries use political influence to gain access to energy supplies.*

*With supplies of gas from the North Sea in decline, we will need more gas storage. If commercial projects are not installed at the predicted rate, or access to storage on the Continent does not materialise, the Government should consider very carefully the case for strategic storage, reserved for emergencies as an insurance policy in an uncertain world. In my judgement, obligations on gas suppliers to ensure that they do supply customers with whom they have contracts also need to be strengthened.*

*For the UK we conclude that total energy independence is not feasible and, indeed, there are advantages through interdependence. However, we must do much more to develop indigenous and alternative energy resources, ranging from new nuclear to renewables, to a rigorous look at exploring anew Britain's own coal reserves, in innovative and clean ways. I recommend that an aspiration that nuclear should provide some 35-40% of our electricity beyond 2030 should be considered by Government. We must also attack vigorously energy inefficiencies with the clear aim of reducing overall energy demand in the United Kingdom. This will also bring significant business opportunities and potentially new skilled employment. All Departments must be seized by the national priority of pursuing urgently these objectives.*

*Notwithstanding such measures, Britain will continue to be heavily reliant on imports in the medium term. We are already relatively well-placed and diversity of supply is crucial. There can be no over-reliance on any one region, country, energy source or pipeline. Building up relationships with key countries is important and the EU needs to be far more proactive in developing specific pipeline infrastructures and electricity connection that will benefit Europe as a whole.*

*Government has recognised the importance of energy for our country's national security in the National Security Strategy 2009. It needs to ensure that energy security is treated with the same focus as other national security issues. To enable this, I recommend that the Government consider setting up an Office of International Energy, bringing together more closely those working across Government on these issues.[50]*

[MW's account of his post-Ministerial career ends here. In 2010, he fought his last General Election campaign. Against the national trend, which enabled David Cameron's Conservatives to form a coalition Government with Nick Clegg's Liberal Democrats, he improved Labour's share of the vote in Croydon North on an increased turnout.

*2010 General Election Result, Croydon North*

| Party | Candidate | Votes | % | +/-% |
| --- | --- | --- | --- | --- |
| Labour | Malcolm WICKS | 28,947 | 56.0 | +2.4 |
| Conservative | Jason HADDEN | 12,466 | 24.1 | +1.9 |
| Liberal Democrat | Gerry JEROME | 7,226 | 14.0 | -3.2 |
| Green | Shasha KHAN | 1,017 | 2.0 | -0.9 |
| UKIP | Jonathan SERTER | 891 | 1.7 | -0.0 |
| Christian | Novelette WILLIAMS | 586 | 1.1 | n/a |
| Respect | Mohommad SHAIKH | 272 | 0.5 | n/a |
| Communist | Ben STEVENSON | 160 | 0.3 | n/a |
| Independent | Mohamed SEYED | 111 | 0.2 | n/a |
| | **Majority** | 16,481 | 31.9 | +0.5 |
| | **Turnout** | 51,676 | 60.6 | +8.0 |

# PART 2

# My Ideas

# 1.

## *What Ministers Do*

Having been a minister in three different departments for a period of over nine years (1999–2008),[51] during the Blair, and briefly, the Brown Governments, I thought it might be useful to reflect on what ministers actually do, their functions, and how they spend their days. In thinking about what I did as a minister, I have avoided going back to some of the classic constitutional texts on what ministers supposedly do, how they are accountable and such like. I am sure there is good literature on this from political scientists and constitutionalists, but I have avoided influencing my own views and approach by consulting these texts.

There are, in addition, numerous accounts by past ministers, often Cabinet Ministers, about their own life and times which shed light on this subject, although they tend understandably to focus on the highlights, the big issues, and the inevitable personality conflicts. My own approach has been more practical, more empirical. It is based, of course, on personal experience. Doubtless other ministers in different departments, say foreign affairs or defence, would give a different account of what ministers do. I can only go by my own experience in education, social security, science, and energy policy.

There are, of course, the rather bold and exciting things that ministers do – passing legislation, making major policy statements, participating in great controversies and so on. I include some of this in my own account, but I also note the more practical, the more day-to-day, some might say the more mundane. Perhaps I have tried to be more anthropological, if that is the term that I am searching for.

In what follows, I have done my best, and as honestly as I can, to note what I actually did. This is not the place for a detailed analysis of the policies I was involved in, but rather my intention is to categorise and illustrate activities. I hope I have avoided grandiose claims, or indeed any claims that do not relate to the truth. The reader, of course, will be the judge. If anything, however, I think that by relaying the day-to-day functions of the minister, for example the endless signing of letters, I may make the job sound more routine than the reader might expect. That is all to the good.

## NB: Ministers are MPs too

The first thing to acknowledge is that ministers are also Members of Parliament (MPs), most of course (about 85%), as elected MPs of the House of Commons, the remainder as Peers in the House of Lords. As a minister, I never forgot that I was also an MP and always sought to remind my civil servants and private office that this was the case. In practical terms it meant that I could not devote 100 per cent of my week to being a minister. I was elected by the people of Croydon North to serve them and this meant a schedule of meetings in the constituency, and generally keeping in touch. The reality was that I could not be such an active constituency MP as I was before I was a minister, but it was important to work hard and maintain links. Having a High Street shop-front office, with experienced staff, helped enormously.

There was one practical implication of this dual role as MP and minister. It meant that on a regular basis I was meeting large numbers of consumers of public policy. Indeed, unlike the senior civil servants in my departments, including the Permanent Secretary, I held advice surgeries regularly, normally on a weekly basis, where I met constituents who had concerns to discuss with me. This certainly kept my feet on the ground. I always felt that, if I was only a minister, as is the case in the United States, for example, and in many other European countries, I would have been more detached. One practical example: when I was Minister for Pensions, responsible for the roll-out of Pension Credit, I was eager to make the process of claiming the means-tested Pension Credit as painless as possible. The application form was redesigned and simplified and, in addition, we established a new Pensions Service. This included a freephone telephone number, so that elderly people (or someone on their behalf) could apply in this way. I was rather proud of what we were doing, but one concerned elderly person came to my surgery and told me straight (she had no idea that I was the Minister for Pensions) that the system was too confusing and too complex and she didn't know how to go about claiming! "Have you seen this application form?" she asked. Regarding these face-to-face issues of social policy, I think I had my finger more on the pulse, and was certainly getting more angry feedback, than my senior civil servants.

For me at least, the constituency work served a wider purpose: it reminded me (should I need reminding) why I was in politics. Again, to note the experience in much of Europe, if I was a full-time minister, being driven around in a government car, working in a smart office, and meeting foreign delegations etc, etc, I might run the risk of getting totally out of touch and beginning to believe that the changes underway had already built Jerusalem in Britain's green and pleasant land.

Yet in the advice surgery, confronted, say, by the mother in constant battle with bureaucrats to get a decent education for a child with special needs, or meeting the family years away from decent housing, or the boy who had been mugged three times in the last year, the reality was different. I thought of these face-to-face experiences as maintaining my 'anger' threshold. This did not mean my shouting and screaming, but rather that I never forgot that Britain was still a society with more than its fair share of injustice and inequality, and consequently with significant numbers of people for whom life was tough, a constant struggle, and full of sadness.

There is, in addition, another aspect of being both an MP and a minister which is worth noting. Constitutionally, of course, ministers are responsible to Parliament and often have to report back to it. As a Member of Parliament oneself, one knew the sheer importance of this, and certainly being in the Chamber on a regular basis meant that one was fully aware that if you got this role wrong you were in deep trouble.

*Ministers are busy*

One fundamental fact about ministerial life is that it is an exceedingly busy one. I reckon that I have worked hard throughout my career, but never so hard as during my period as minister. These things are difficult to calculate, but I reckon I worked at least an 80-hour week. Starting times in the morning varied, but if there was a flight planned, to Manchester, Aberdeen, or Brussels, one was out of bed far too early, and certainly on Mondays and Tuesdays, when the House of Commons typically votes at 10pm, you could chalk up a 15-hour day without really trying. The House of Commons votes earlier on Wednesdays and Thursdays and so the week gets a bit easier, but there were still often evening engagements. Friday through to Sunday consisted of juggling constituency engagements, including the critical advice surgery, with the inevitable need to do five or more hours' work on the red boxes that sat in the corner of my study at home.

In preparation for a talk to civil servants about what ministers do, I asked my Private Secretary for a rough estimate of the volume of work that came in under various headings. This was in 2007, when the Commons was in session. The results are detailed in Table 1. It shows that the number of documents crammed into my ministerial box each month numbered some 1,200. These would vary from perhaps just two sheets drawing a matter to my attention, through to some twenty pages or more relating to a statutory instrument, detailing secondary legislation that later comes before a House committee. Again I stress that the minister's experience will vary from department to department and I can only present my own experience. Certainly in the Department for Work & Pensions (DWP) there were many, many more letters to sign off, most to other MPs writing in about constituency benefit cases. (I can see now why it was, occasionally, the custom for one staff member to sit on the box as the only way possible for another to lock it.)

So life was busy, but I also received fantastic support from the civil service in general and, in particular, from my Private Office. At Minister of State level this would consist, typically, of four, normally quite young officials, headed up by a Private Secretary. Although not always, she or he would often be a 'fast track' civil servant, not very long out of university. The main roles of the Private Office would be to process the mass of work that came in, in order that the minister would only see that which was important, and also to act as the vital point of communications between the minister, the wider department, and the rest of the Whitehall machine. Private office staff worked long hours and, in my experience, could not do enough to help the minister.

It could be tough and sometimes brave work: often denying access to officials who felt that their subject warranted disrupting an already bursting day; or chasing up senior officials to enquire where the promised submission had got to; or reminding their colleagues that not every delayed paper would get into the weekend box (there being those who felt they needn't get their work to the minister until as late as possible in the week, no doubt assuming that, despite their dilatoriness, he would be delighted to read their thoughts at 10pm on a Sunday evening).

Another key support was the driver allocated through the Government Car Service. Mick was my driver for over nine years and I simply couldn't have done the job as well without him. He would pick me up in the morning, be available throughout the day, driving me home at night.

*Table 1: One minister's workload (2007)*

|  | Daily | Monthly★ |
|---|---|---|
| Letters to send | 15 | 300 |
| Written Parliamentary Questions | 13 | 260 |
| Formal submissions | 25 | 500 |
| E-mails received | 110 | 2200 |
| Total physical documents in box | 60 | 1200 |
| Engagements (including debates etc) | 10 | 200 |
| **In the last two weeks:** |  |  |
| Parliamentary debates | 5 |  |
| Speeches | 14 |  |

★ Monthly totals based on 5 working days per week, 20 working days per month.

Coming in I would be able to do up to an hour's work on the box, while lending half an ear to Radio 4's Today programme. It was a very effective office on wheels. (No doubt influenced by the MPs' expenses scandal and by the climate of austerity, the car service has been much reduced and ministers no longer get the service that was so vital to my work. Taking cars away from ministers might be good politics, but it must make for less effective government.)

*The work of a minister*

I categorise my work as a minister under broad headings – an ambassadorial role; an authoriser of decisions; accountability to parliament; and policy making and implementation.

*An ambassadorial role*

The minister is a key spokesperson, a kind of ambassador for both his/her department and the wider government. This role is shared, of course, with other ministers, and indeed with all civil servants at different levels. It is a function that you undertake at both home and abroad. It involves getting around the UK and, with certain portfolios, more internationally; doing a great deal of listening; and also, of course, a fair share of speechifying. Some commentators, from a suitably lofty position, might say that most of these meetings were a waste of time. Some might be, but it is important to allow access and avoid the charge that one is aloof in the Whitehall office.

In some ministerial portfolios the giving of speeches is an onerous burden. Sometimes I would be called upon to give three or so a day, some long, some happily short. As you get to know your subject you can ad lib more and more, and if the speech is only ten minutes or so long, it is better to throw away the official note and do it on the hoof. It is important to inject your own personality into even the driest of speeches. I would try and articulate my own narrative, tell my own story, about the challenges and policy objectives. But if the subject is complex and detailed, you more or less have to stick to the official script. I hated that and was never happy reading out a ten- or fifteen-page speech. I didn't think I was very good at it and kept trying to get myself into the speech somehow, by ad libbing (either appropriately or inappropriately).

Some civil servants are rather good at writing speeches and get to know the minister's style. One civil servant at the DWP, Paul Howarth, having listened to me once or twice mangling the speech that he had written for me, with my own interjections all over the place, next time presented me with a speech that was so like me that

I thought that I must have written it myself. That kind of thing helps a great deal.

*Mass media*

This ambassadorial, or spokesman, role is critical when it comes to the media. Sometimes the department can do its best to control the presentation of policy to the media. A publication day for a new document would be set; a news release developed; and, on a good day, ten or so interviews would take place, from early morning with Radio 4's Today programme, through to BBC's Newsnight, although often the story would have run out of steam by early afternoon. On a bad day, despite the most careful planning and presentation, the subject would fail totally to take off. While some ministers did their best to avoid it, I always rather enjoyed the semi-gladiatorial contests with the likes of Jeremy Paxman and Jon Snow.

On other occasions, of course, invitations to appear on the media were not so welcome. Something had gone wrong, a power station was out of action perhaps, or a business or non-governmental organisation (NGO) had made unhelpful comments about policy.

With any luck, the Minister can be well-prepared for a media interview, but often one was skating on thin ice. In 2005, and just four or five days after being appointed Minister for Energy, a subject that I was not well-versed in following four years at the DWP, I was invited onto Newsnight to discuss nuclear energy. I think I did alright but I was rather conscious that I was only thirty seconds or so away from revealing my ignorance. Again, within days of being appointed Energy Minister, I was on Radio 4's Today programme to discuss carbon capture and storage (CCS). Later I became a great champion of CCS and got to know what I was talking about, but not on this occasion. My having explained that CCS involved the stripping out of $CO_2$ from fossil-fuel power stations and then transporting the $CO_2$ through pipelines to the depleted oil or gas reservoir offshore in the North Sea,

I was asked (and it was a perfectly reasonable question) "is the $CO_2$ liquefied?"; I had absolutely no idea and replied, "something like that". My wife was in despair, but a senior civil servant, back at HQ, was positive and she told me that the answer "something like that" was about right.

Some interviews take place in rather peculiar circumstances. Once, while Science Minister, during a trip to Antarctica, we spent a night out on the ice, under canvas. I had agreed, perhaps rather too enthusiastically, to do a radio interview with the BBC World Service. But this involved waking up at about 4am in the morning, icy winds roaring, alarm clock blazing, putting on a head torch, and then dialling an extraordinarily long number on a special satellite phone. I was rather amazed when I got a clear answer: "This is the BBC World Service". Lord Oxburgh, who was sharing the tent was, I assumed, asleep throughout the interview. But the next morning he regaled our party with how he had had a most peculiar dream, involving a government minister talking to the BBC at some unearthly hour.

On another occasion in Qatar I was invited on to Al Jazeera. The interview was to be part of a live news bulletin. The questions would be asked in Arabic, but the interpreter would be standing just outside the studio, relaying the questions to me, via an earpiece, in English. I immediately felt uneasy: this could go very badly wrong. Fortunately they outlined four questions they would ask me in advance. The programme duly started with a rousing musical fanfare and so it came to my interview. The first question was asked, but by way of interpretation all I could hear was a low mumbling, with the occasional words—'energy', 'global', 'UK'—that I understood. It would have disrupted the programme to say that I could hardly hear anything and so, vaguely remembering the ground they wanted to cover, I just started talking for a minute or two and then waited for the next question. Again the mumbling came through the earpiece, but by then I was in my stride and just tried to make intelligent statements which the presenters seemed very happy with. Come to think of it, it was not so different from any other interview, because you always try to get key messages across whatever the questions being asked!

*The minister as an authoriser of decisions*

This makes the minister sound like a mere rubber stamp and is a description that appeals to all cynics who think that ministers are somehow superfluous and simply do what their civil servants tell them. This is not what I mean. The point, however, is that a great mass of documentation reaches the minister every day, every week. Table 1 shows the volume. This documentation follows the minister around in the famous red boxes, a kind of departmental stalker, carried home at night in the back of the official car and accompanying you home at weekends – often not one box, but two or three.

The official papers come in all shapes and sizes, much of them relatively routine, some of enormous importance. They include replies to MPs who have written to the minister, usually about constituency cases, which have to be authorised and signed by the minister. They also include Statutory Instruments, highly technical and dull documents, which the minister has to agree and which may well, some months later, be the subject of a committee hearing. MPs put down numerous Parliamentary Questions (PQs), and while the answers are drafted by civil servants, they have to be agreed (and if not agreed, then amended) by the Minister. At Energy, there were also planning decisions and authorisations that required the formal yea or nay of the minister, most controversially often about the location of wind farms. (A proposed wind farm off Cardigan Bay might prove a threat to dolphins, some environmentalists argued. Local primary schools took up the campaign and, for several weeks, the office was deluged with children's pretty pictures of these creatures.) There would also be numerous official submissions about up and coming policy matters. Ministers would be asked for a decision or a strong 'steer' about direction.

Ministers are also on several Ministerial groups or official Cabinet committees, often involving policy areas far removed from the day-to-day functions of the Minister. For example, for a year or two I was the Departmental Minister on the Cross-Ministerial Committee looking at the likely threat of avian flu. (How serious was the threat? What was the incidence in Asia at present? How many vaccines should be ordered? And were the vaccines available fit for purpose, given that likely strains of flu could not be determined until they hit? If the incidence turned out to be a very serious one (as it may well do in the future), how would one cope with the rising mortality levels, what were the practical implications for burials and cremations?) These committees are important if cross-departmental approaches are to develop, something that government has become better at in recent times.

A close working relationship with another department is sometimes essential. The best example from my time at Energy was the work of DEFRA (Department for Environment, Food and Rural Affairs), the department with responsibility for climate change. Their ministers and I worked well together, but there was an inevitable tension between DEFRA's aim to reduce $CO_2$ levels and the energy imperative of ensuring power at not too high a price.

So the Minister has to wade through this documentation which, certainly at the weekends, when the red boxes were unlocked, could be several feet tall. If family and sleep were not to be altogether sacrificed, the Minister has to make careful judgements. What can be quickly scanned and authorised? Is it really necessary to read through and check every ministerial reply to an MP (although if the letter turns out to be a dud the consequences to reputation with colleagues could be serious)? Is it vital to read that speech on tidal power given that it will not be delivered for a day or two? And how to deal with most of the box quickly, in order that more time can be devoted to that important policy submission about the future of the low carbon economy?

A critique that could be levelled at ministers is that they routinely undertake work – signing off letters, authorising minor decisions, etc – that is simply that – routine. No CEO of a major company would go anywhere near those chores. No doubt some improvements could be made, but such criticism fails to understand the nature of ministerial accountability, and crucially the fact that, while civil servants advise, ministers must make the decisions.

The task of the private office is to ensure that the Minister deals with every last piece of paper as soon as possible. I always felt the task of the Minister was to do his/her best without going mad! I know ministers who would diligently work into the early hours of the morning to finish their box. I sometimes judged that an hour's extra sleep would be of more service to the nation, even if that provoked a disappointed look from a 25-year-old Private Secretary!

Once, during a summer recess, I was working at home and the red box had duly been delivered. I looked around for the box key. It was nowhere to be found and so I rang the private office to see if I'd left it on my desk. My diary manager answered: yes indeed I had left it on the desk, but he had safeguarded it like the good civil servant that he was. "So where's the key now?" "Don't worry, Malcolm, I put it in the box". And then, when I enquired what he did next, he said: "I locked the box". A short silence followed, during which I could hear the penny dropping, and then the most plaintive cries which seemed to last a long time – "ooooooooooooooooooohhhhh".

A Minister's time is pressured and precious. When I was a young university teacher, I would worry away at a lecture weeks in advance – checking the literature, updating statistics etc. As a Minister, I would find it difficult to focus on a speech until the day before its delivery, or on the morning, if it was an afternoon engagement. This might not be good, but it is how it is.

*Accountability to Parliament*

As noted above, the Minister is also likely to be an MP in the House of Commons, and the importance of the constitutional function of Ministerial accountability should take on a practical meaning for the MP, and not just a formal one. You are performing in front of your Parliamentary colleagues and they can be harsh and certainly shrewd observers and critics. And that's just on your own side, let alone the Opposition!

This Parliamentary accountability takes many forms. There will be PQs that need answering, some on the floor of the House of Commons itself during departmental questions that takes place every three or four weeks or so. You will not be alone, but there with your ministerial colleagues. One may only have one or two questions to answer, but depending on the subject, sometimes far more. The Secretary of State will choose a few questions to answer, from the range of the departmental portfolio. The minister receives ample briefing from the civil service, but sometimes this is too narrow. Civil servants are not always a good judge of the political climate (and party politics is not their affair) or aware of a recent incident in the constituency that might be raised by the Member. The minister's political antennae are vital here. Even the most innocuous question might prompt supplementaries from other MPs about related, sometimes not very related, issues or recent incidents or tragedies. The minister therefore needs to be fully aware of context, not least political, and also has to be quick-witted and fast on his or her feet. Sometimes you simply do not know the answer to a supplementary question, particularly if it is a very technical one, and the minister has to judge how to handle this. The well-known formula of promising to write to the Honourable Member can normally get you out of a hole.

In addition to oral questions taken in the Chamber, there are far, far more written questions that require answers. Again these need to be authorised by the Minister. Over the last decade or two the number of written questions has grown in volume, no doubt aided by the somewhat better staffing resourcing available to backbench MPs and also to the fact that numerous interest groups, business bodies, NGOs etc etc, seek to persuade backbenchers to ask questions on their behalf. In the year 2000–1, an average of 200 written questions were put down each day; by 2009–10 that number had doubled. For the session 2010–12 (up to 23 March), over 93,000 questions had been answered. Some MPs, particularly I think from the newer intakes, seek to ask bucket loads of questions, no doubt to impress their constituents (and themselves). These are often the handiwork of eager, unpaid interns and the cost to the taxpayer is not insignificant.

*Select committees*

Since their early origins, associated with Richard Crossman in the 1960s, and Norman St John Stevas in the early 1980s, departmental select committees have grown in importance, and an appearance before one is among the most demanding things that a minister can experience. I have been on both sides of the fence: I served on the then Social Security Select Committee earlier on in my parliamentary career, and for one year was Chair of the Select Committee on Education. I was therefore used to questioning and scrutinising ministers, senior civil servants, and other key actors from universities, NGOs, and business. As a minister I frequently had to appear before departmental select committees. Answering the questions is far more demanding than merely asking them! The session might last one and a half or even two hours, you are asked detailed points, and you need to know your stuff. It was one function I took most seriously and did my homework for, with very thorough briefings from my civil servants. A senior official might testify with you and answer some questions, but it is best for the minister to take most of the flak. It is perhaps the most serious testing of ministerial accountability – the Commons at its most grown-up and normally relatively nonpartisan – and one I most enjoyed, especially when it was over.

In addition to appearances before select committees, the minister might be asked to attend other Commons' and, indeed, House of Lords' committees. Parliament is also littered with All-Party Parliamentary Groups (APPGs) representing an extraordinary wide range of interests. In the year 2011, 559 APPGs were officially registered. In my experience APPGs are something of a misnomer. Sometimes relatively few MPs or Lords attend but the room can be chock-a-block full of representatives of industry, some academics, and numerous representatives of NGOs. They can be, however, an important channel into parliament.

One day I had spoken at one APPG on green issues and needed to leave quickly to attend another meeting back in the department. Just before I left there was one more question. The questioner announced, somewhat grandly, that he was writing a book and he asked when did I think peak oil would occur. (I should explain that 'peak oil', in my experience, attracts a certain kind of adherent who approaches the question in an almost theological way, rather than empirically as surely should be the case.) Obviously peak oil, and gas too, will occur at some point, but no-one knows when and much depends on new geological finds (there is now shale gas to contend with, for example), what the environmental costs of extraction are and the financial costs too, compared with, say, new nuclear or renewables. But all that is too rational for the adherents. I had no time to give a proper answer to the question and, collecting my papers to leave, said that I thought peak oil would occur on August 29th but I didn't know which year! Some were kind enough to recognise my attempt at humour but, as I was to find out later, not the questioner. Indeed in his book[52] he devoted a whole chapter, 'Memo to Mr Wicks', to our encounter: "Leaving aside the gratuitous put-down and the generally fatuous tone, Mr Wicks's reply demonstrated apparently bullet-proof ignorance of the basics of oil depletion".

I always rather felt that some in the green movement should learn to laugh a bit more.

*Policy-making*

*The context: hearing the voices*

Before discussing different aspects of policy-making, let me note the context within which the Minister operates. Ministers do not work in a vacuum, and policies do not come out of thin air. It is rare to start with a clean sheet. Rather policies are formulated, rationally or less so, within the context of often great complexity. And also against the backcloth of history – for example, National Insurance was first legislated for in 1911; much education policy also has a rich history. Economics and finance, administrative realities, existing legislation and the courts, party policy and public opinion, science and research, sectional interests, pressure groups, the media, and so much more, all play their part.

Ministers therefore do not operate in the dark or in the quiet. Rather they are subject, sometimes it seems, victims, of a cacophony of voices. Everyone with an interest in their subject – pensions, energy, education etc – has to have their say. Some are genuine experts and I always respected the academic community. That was my background and I was never shy, in my pre-political career, to present policy proposals, criticise the governments of the day, both Labour and Conservative, and generally give my point of view, sometimes based on sound research, sometimes, I guess, based more on my values and political opinions. I therefore recognise the strength of academic opinion, but also its susceptibilities and weaknesses. Few weigh up the public expenditure consequences of their pronouncements. They lack knowledge of how to turn a good idea into a specific proposal and the consequences for administration. In recent times, however, more academics have been employed by government – as advisers, report writers etc, and this has led to less of a divide between government and academia.

Academics are just one group of key actors. Indeed there is a vast and increasing army of 'experts' – from industry, the professions, claimants, and customers, and an array of NGOs, charities, and interest groups of all shapes and sizes – clear and often shrill about their demands and the over-riding importance of their own particular subject.

The challenge was to determine which experts were not simply in the business of representing their own interests or views, whether they were from industry, the NGO sector, or academia, but could also give you a more objective and honest account of the situation. Fortunately these people existed and were always the ones I listened to carefully. The others I was polite enough to give the time of day to, but was pleased when they went on their way.

Secretaries of State are allowed three or so special advisers, known inelegantly as SpAds. They tend to be a mixture of genuine experts in their subject and 'politicos' who advise on presentation and party matters. The Minister of State has no special advisers but has access to them, and I found that they often provided a valuable source of advice and direction. As Pensions Minister it was our SpAds, Tom Clark and Chris Norton, who played a key role in developing ideas for both the Pension Protection Fund and the Financial Assistance Scheme.

Some experts make extravagant claims about themselves. I sometimes had the impression that all it needed was for someone to walk down Downing Street once in their lives, for them to become, ever more, a 'former number 10 Downing Street adviser'.

There is no end of opportunity for the Minister to hear the voices all too ready to advise him. And this is a positive. It is important to speak not only to civil servants, and fellow ministers, but to a wide variety of interests and viewpoints. It is vital, however, not to let the last meeting and the last lobbying session bear too much of an imprint on one's own view and the direction one was set upon.

The Engineering Employers' Federation, a body I respected, lobbied me several times. When I was Pensions Minister during the period 2003 to 2005, they showed up in some state of agitation and told me that the pensions question was now the key issue for the boards of directors of their member companies. A year or so later Tony Blair moved me to the energy portfolio. The Federation sought an early meeting: "Minister, we want you to understand that energy costs are the key issue of concern to our boards of directors". I think I was undiplomatic enough to say, "Hang on a minute. That's what you told me last year about pensions!" "Well Minister", they countered, "last year it was pensions". I started to understand how their meetings with ministers for schools, vocational education, business and science would start off. But to be fair, both portfolios were hot ones.

### The protestors

Most representations from interest groups are conducted, civilly, usually around the ministerial table. In addition, however, there were the more colourful demonstrations and protests.

While Pensions Minister, I always enjoyed my encounters with the so-called 'pensioners' movement'. It taught me however to ask a question, if only to myself, "who do you represent and who do you exclude?" Crucially who are the 'silent voices' and how do we recognise their needs? The fact that the leading members of the movement were very often former shop stewards, of Communist or Trotskyite persuasion, suggested to me that they were not altogether typical of elderly people across the country. They were shocked if you voiced this possibility. They invariably demanded a rise in the basic state pension and hated the idea of means-testing. Both propositions were ones I had every sympathy for, but the harsh reality was that putting all of our resources into the National Insurance pension would benefit many people, like the leaders of the so-called movement, who also had income from occupational pensions – former teachers and other public servants, those working on the buses and trains, and other wellunionised areas of industry where the works pension had been enshrined. They did not represent often quite elderly people, in their 80s and 90s, mainly women, who did not benefit from these occupational pensions and needed some extra support, which the Labour Government sought to deliver through the new pension credit.

## The policy cycle

To explain ministerial involvement in policy and legislation, the idea of the policy cycle is useful. The starting point is the regular need to think and review, usually because existing policy is no longer fit for purpose (events have intervened or a new government has new ideas) or, less commonly, a 'new' issue now demands government attention. Examples include the growing concern about obesity in the last decade, cyber terrorism, and internet pornography.

Having reviewed the subject and policy options, it is time to move towards decision-making, probably following consultations and perhaps the publication of a Green Paper. There might then be a policy statement in the form of a White Paper and / or a ministerial statement or, if important enough, a prime ministerial speech. Next might be the need for new legislation, if policy requires a fresh legal underpinning. Once a new Act of Parliament has been secured, detailed implementation is required. Later there will be another review. This presents a somewhat idealistic version as sometimes 'events', perhaps a sudden scandal or tragedy, leads to hasty action' – for good or ill. However it largely accords with my experience.

Most ministers would see policy-making as an essential activity. Indeed, whatever their political values, it is often why they got into politics in the first place – to get things done. Most ministers, however, quickly discover that it's not so simple. They are not presented with the luxury of a blank sheet of paper. Although never blank, the nearest they might get to that is after a general election when a new government is formed – a 1997 or 2010 moment. Even then, of course, policy cannot be developed in a vacuum: there are likely to be many years, indeed several decades of policy-making, including legislation, already in place. So the idea that the new and idealistic minister can immediately change the world according to his or her lights is a naïve one. Nevertheless, opportunities do arise to think afresh about policy and any sensible minister will seize on these.

The policy timescale is likely to be several years from initial thoughts and review to implementation and indeed is likely to be longer, often far longer, than the Minister's own term in that particular job. Similarly, many civil servants are likely to have moved on during that period. In principle such rapid movement of both ministers and civil servants should not matter greatly because of 'institutional memory'. I fear that that 'memory', while existing hopefully in digital files, is rather overstated. I remember, while at the Department for Education & Employment (DfEE), asking the civil servants responsible for Education Action Zones how these related to the Educational Priority Areas that were introduced following the Plowden Report of 1967. They were bright officials, but they stared at me blankly: they had no idea what I was talking about. And yet that earlier experience of priority areas, not just in education but more widely, would have been highly relevant to not dissimilar exercises undertaken by the Labour Government.

Let me give examples of different stages of the policy cycle – review, legislation, and implementation.

*Review*

I was appointed Minister of State for Energy by Tony Blair in 2005. Several months later the Prime Minister decided that a new review of energy policy should be undertaken, primarily to settle the question as to whether or not the UK should build a new generation of nuclear reactors. For the Labour Party this was a controversial issue, with many backbenchers and party supporters instinctively opposed to nuclear energy. Opposition from key ministers, including Margaret Beckett and

Michael Meacher in the environment department, had stood in the way of policy movement, leaving the government sitting on an uncomfortable fence.

How to conduct the review? Different options were presented: some favoured appointing an outsider to do the work, others wanted to take it out of the department and assign the role to the Cabinet Office. The department itself, of course, wanted to take responsibility and it was a relief to me that Tony Blair asked me to lead the review, something that my then Secretary of State, Alan Johnson, supported. A review team of officials was put together, analysis undertaken, many were consulted, and we published a report in January 2006.[53] We reviewed the challenges facing Britain's energy needs and the contribution different energy sources might play and how these relate to key challenges in energy supply and climate change. Our central recommendation however, and certainly the one that caused most controversy, was that Britain should allow a new generation of nuclear reactors to be constructed. A week may sometimes be a long time in politics, but the challenges of both climate change and energy security demand the long-term view. Parliament has now legislated for an 80 per cent $CO_2$ reduction by 2050 and any new nuclear reactors are unlikely to be operating this side of 2020.

Another policy opportunity presented itself to me at the DWP when, as a Parliamentary Under-Secretary of State, I had responsibility for Housing Benefit. This is a complex area of public policy and expenditure on Housing Benefit had increased substantially in recent years. The Prime Minister and others supported reform but the precise nature was unclear. There was a policy impasse. My major concern was the privately rented sector where, all too often, the Housing Benefit was simply sent from the local council to the landlord, so disempowering the tenant. It certainly offered no encouragement to the tenant to move elsewhere in search of better accommodation or put pressure on the landlord for improvements.

Working closely with the DWP team of officials, a smart and

determined bunch, we hammered out a new strategy and developed the idea of a housing allowance that would normally be paid direct to the tenant. This in itself was controversial, not least with the private landlord interest, who had grown used to receiving the payments direct and no doubt felt that they had some kind of inalienable right to receive this tranche of taxpayers' money. There were, of course, more legitimate concerns that some tenants, including those on the margins of society, possibly suffering from drink or other addiction problems, would simply fail to pay the landlord the rent, choosing instead to spend the money on no doubt more immediate pleasures. So we had a provision that in these kinds of cases the allowance would still be paid direct to the landlord. For me, as minister, this was an example of a policy that I was able to help fashion and see through to a pilot stage with a plan that could be thoroughly tested. An idea to extend the housing allowance approach to the council and social housing sector ran into the barrier of traditionalism in parts of the Labour Government.

## Legislation

Legislation is a detailed, complex, and time-consuming operation. It requires moving from, often relatively broadbrush, policy intention, to the detailed provisions of primary legislation (a Bill leading to an Act of Parliament) and, yet more detailed, the possible need for secondary, or delegated, legislation. Enter the lawyers and Parliamentary Counsel whose task it is to turn ministerial and departmental intentions into legislative precision. All of this requires winning parliamentary time, competing against other departments for the right to get your bill into a crowded legislative schedule. And persuading a ministerial committee – the L Committee – that your bill is in good shape to withstand scrutiny by the Commons and their Lordships. If time is secured, the graft really starts. Most bills start in the Commons, a minority in the Lords. There will be a Second Reading debate, kicked off by the Secretary of State, an occasion where broad measures are outlined and where crude politics flexes its muscles, often more an occasion for the partisan than the policy analyst.

## Committee Stage

During my term in office I had responsibility for three major parliamentary bills (and a few smaller ones) which became the Learning & Skills Act of 2000, the Pensions Act of 2004, and the Energy Act, 2008. All were demanding, intricate measures.

The Committee Stage of the bill is arguably the most testing (and fatiguing) challenge for a minister. The department will establish a Bill Team, a cadre of officials dedicated to getting the bill through Parliament. The team will be supported by more civil servants who will appear at committee when their subject is up for scrutiny. The officials present cannot speak, of course, but their job is to detect when the Minister needs more information and when he needs to answer a specific question.

If answering a PQ in the Chamber can be likened to a quick sprint, and a select committee hearing to a tough 5,000 metres, then the Committee Stage of a bill is very much a marathon. The Pensions Bill 2004 ended up with 325 sections in the final published Act, plus 13 schedules. It involved 22 separate committee sittings, usually two on a Tuesday and two more on a Thursday. The committee's work lasted from 9 March to 27 April.

The schedule of meetings required a busy weekend studying a large volume of papers detailing issues and questions clause by clause. The Monday required more reading and meetings with the Bill Team, often focusing on Opposition amendments that could be tabled quite late. The Tuesday would be dominated by the two committee sessions, perhaps lasting up to five hours in total; the Wednesday brought more briefings, and Thursday, two more sessions. It all entailed a dedicated focus on the legislation, albeit that other engagements, including parliamentary appearances, and other paperwork, had to be fitted in around the bill.

This work I found to be among the most rewarding part of my ministerial career. There was a clear objective, an excellent team backing you, and one just needed the stamina and humour to plough through to reach the end.

The Pensions Act was particularly challenging. We were clear about our objectives – to establish a Pension Protection Fund (so that when companies went bust, workers and existing company pensioners would not have to lose most of their pensions) and a Pensions Regulator (to bring financial integrity and discipline to the sector) – but our Bill was far from being in a perfect state, as Parliamentary Counsel sought to remind us. All other things being equal, the bill should have been delayed a year, but things were not equal: people's pensions were being lost and we had to act fast. This meant that we amended our own bill almost 1,000 times – a near record! This may not have been the legislative process at its finest, but it was social reform at its best.

## Policy implementation

Very often the minister new to a department will discover the policy is already established, that the key decisions have been made – the White Paper is published, the legislation is in place – and that his or her task is to see the policy through to successful implementation. This, in fact, can be a more challenging task than simply setting out policy strategy. The devil is certainly in the detail and successful implementation will often depend not on the government itself, but on several different agencies and institutions, some in the public sector, others in the private sphere.

At DWP the policy for pension credit was already in place when I became Pensions Minister in June 2003. As noted earlier, I was not by instinct a means-tester, but I recognised the need to get more money into the hands of the very elderly. My job was to make implementation a success. I set up a steering group that met regularly; we looked at issues in great detail and monitored take-up rates. My senior officials may have felt that I was getting too involved in administration – their role, not mine. But I had no doubt that successful implementation was crucial and that I needed to get involved in the fine detail.

An example from my time in DfEE concerned adult basic skills, a euphemism deployed to summarise the fact that many adults in the UK had somehow survived the primary and secondary education system without learning to adequately read, write, or understand basic arithmetic. This, of course, is a human tragedy, lives blunted as a consequence, in terms of access to employment, career progression, simple day-to-day interactions in shops and elsewhere.

We established a working party of officials, and drew on expertise from both home and abroad. Susan Pember headed the professional team and we spent many hours every week looking at the materials that should be used, asking why existing adult skills classes normally ended in failure for the student,and how we could raise the whole professional game when it came to the teaching experience.

The project met with much success. I came across many adults, later, who had benefited enormously and who are now able to write that letter to a grandchild in Australia or even to pen a memoir about their lives, or simply enjoy reading a book for the first time. Given the daily slog of being a minister, when you sometimes wonder whether all of this work makes a difference, to meet someone in their 60s and 70s who could read or write for the first time is a wonderful experience, a creative human light flashing.

## Conclusion

British politics is at a low ebb. We live in a cynical and suspicious age from which few institutions escape. So let me assert that my own ministerial experience runs counter to this snide current in political discourse.

In every role I undertook I worked with dedicated and competent officials and I felt that we made real progress. At DfEE we developed the Connexions Service which aimed, in particular, to help those children in difficulty have a second or third chance to attain educational achievement. At DWP we pursued Housing Benefit reform, and implemented the Pension Credit campaign, which saw many elderly people gain £30 or more extra a week. We passed the Pensions Act of 2004, so establishing the Pension Protection Fund which safeguards the pensions of over 500,000 people. At Energy we moved forward on renewable energy projects, promoted CCS, and took the decision on nuclear energy.

I am obviously too close to the action to be entirely objective, but my own ministerial experience runs counter to the fashionable and cynical view of government. My experience is that central government can be a major force for good, that things can change for the better, and that lives can be improved and enhanced. Unfashionable perhaps, but it is my testimony.

# Rights, Wrongs and Responsibilities: Citizenship and Social Policy

Among the very many challenges facing the next Labour government will be to rebuild trust in the social security system. This requires some rigorous thinking now, in Opposition. By 2015 the system will be characterised by mass unemployment and low benefit levels. Moreover, after years witnessing the triumph of fear over hope, faith in the welfare state will be at a low level with many benefit claimants on the hostile end of popular attitudes, not least from those in employment whose salaries are in decline.

Faced with this likely legacy, Labour's challenge is not to defend the system circa 2010 but rather to rebuild new public confidence in a system based on rights and duties, a move back towards full employment and sound finance. A tall order, yes, but no more so than that facing the 1945 Attlee Government that moved forward on so many fronts – housing, planning, social security and, of course, the National Health Service. Indeed, we can draw strength from the ambition, idealism and determination of that Labour Government, in the immediate post-war period, when economic circumstances (including the simple shortage of materials for housing) were so much worse than those confronting the Coalition Government now.

## History

Where do we begin? Let me suggest one starting point. We are witnessing the 100th anniversary of the birth of National Insurance: the 1911 National Insurance Act received Royal Assent in December of that year, contributions were first made in July 1912 and the first benefits paid the following January. That early history is associated with illustrious political figures, notably the Liberal, Lloyd George, and also Winston Churchill himself who said:

> *If I had to sum up the immediate future of democratic politics in a single word I should say "Insurance". If I had my way I would write the word "Insure" over the door of every cottage, and upon the blotting book of every public man....*[54]

The 1911 National Insurance Act may have been a modest measure, but it paved the way for radical reform. Later, of course, another famous Liberal, William Beveridge, produced his ground breaking wartime report of 1942[55]. Beveridge spoke graphically, using language that puts contemporary spin doctors to shame, about the challenges that lay ahead:

> *Reconstruction has many sides, international and domestic. On the domestic side one can define its aims best by naming five giants evils to be destroyed – Want, Disease, Ignorance, Squalor and Idleness.*[56]

Following the war the Labour government introduced the National Insurance Act of 1946 and with it unemployment and sickness benefits, old age pensions etc. Beveridge's vision, of course, was never fully enacted. Notably National Insurance benefit levels were often below those of non contributory means tested benefits. And from the late 1960s onwards a powerful and well meaning welfare rights movement (and I was part of it) encouraged take up of these means tested benefits and extended the boundaries of entitlement, but this inevitably undermined the contributory principle.

Profound social changes around divorce and separation,

cohabitation (with relationships often more fragile than marriage) and births outside marriage led to a dramatic increase in the number and proportion of one parent families. In 1961 300,000 dependent children lived with a lone parent, by 2010 it was 1.8 million [Table 1].

*Table 1*

Single family households:[57]                                                          *millions*

by type Great Britain

|  | 1961 | 1971 | 1981 | 1991 | 2001 | 2010 |
|---|---|---|---|---|---|---|
| **One family households** | | | | | | |
| *Couple*[58] | | | | | | |
| No children | 4.2 | 5.0 | 5.3 | 6.3 | 6.9 | 7.1 |
| 1–2 dependent children[59] | 4.9 | 4.8 | 5.1 | 4.5 | 4.5 | 4.6 |
| 3 or more dependent children[59] | 1.3 | 1.7 | 1.2 | 1.1 | 1.0 | 0.8 |
| **Couples with dependent** children | 6.2 | 6.5 | 6.3 | 5.6 | 5.5 | 5.3 |
| Non-dependent children only | 1.6 | 1.5 | 1.6 | 1.8 | 1.4 | 1.5 |
| **Lone parent**[58] | | | | | | |
| Dependent children[59] | 0.3 | 0.6 | 1.0 | 1.3 | 1.7 | 1.8 |
| Non-dependent children only | 0.7 | 0.7 | 0.8 | 0.9 | 0.7 | 0.8 |

Many are dependent on means tested benefits. These trends put huge pressure on the system and raised serious questions about the appropriate balance to be struck between a rights approach, given clear social needs, and a contributory one.

Moreover, a powerful feminist critique portrayed the system, correctly, as one more suited to a man's employment profile than that of a woman. This was partly put right by later Labour governments which legislated for home responsibility payments, crediting in mothers during the period when they were bringing up their children and, later, also recognising the role of carers in the family. However, the lower earnings of women meant that it was only partially remedied, especially as earnings related pensions were extended.

The contributory principle was also undermined by successive governments, both Conservative and Labour, that failed to renew and communicate the social contract that the contributory principle was based upon and depended upon. Indeed those governments increasingly regarded the contributions system as simply another form of taxation. This has been all too apparent in recent times when, during the dying months of the Labour Government, there was an argument between Gordon Brown and Alistair Darling as to whether to raise National Insurance contributions (favoured by Brown) or VAT levels (favoured by Darling). I suspect that during these internal discussions little thought was given to the nature of the contributory principle and what National Insurance was meant to be all about.

Despite all of this, National Insurance still plays a very major role [Table 2]. In 2010/11 contributory payment expenditure was just over £82 billion pounds, some 43% of total social security payments. Income related benefits represented 38% of the total [including tax credits], while non contributory non income related benefits [disability benefits and Child Benefit] represent 19% of the total.

*Table 2*

**UK total – all social security payment expenditure:**

|  | £ million | % of total UK social security payment expenditure | % of total UK government expenditure | % of UK GDP |
|---|---|---|---|---|
| Contributory | 82,358 | 43% | 12% | 6% |
| Income related | 73,362 | 38% | 11% | 5% |
| Non contributory non income related | 37,531 | 19% | 5% | 3% |
| **Total** | **193,252** | **100%** | **28%** | **13%** |
| UK Total Managed Expenditure | 687,800 | | | |
| Gross Domestic Product at current Market prices (ONS series YBHA) | 1,478,417 | | | |

I believe firmly that the ethical, political and financial case for the contributory principle remains strong and coherent. Yet it is undoubtedly in a state of disrepair, faded and jaded.

Now is therefore a good opportunity, a century on, to re-evaluate the purpose of National Insurance, and to ask the question 'does

National Insurance have any real relevance in contemporary Britain and in particular can the contributory principle still serve as a foundation stone for a modern social security system?'.

*Values*

The starting point, as we seek to develop coherent and affordable policies for the future, must be our values. our underlying beliefs that shape our key principles.

What are the key values? Well, a good starting point, as ever, are the values of the French Revolution – liberté, égalité, fraternité: I would argue that these are guided by three key principles:

- we must aim for a more equal society;
- it must be one that liberates individuals and families, empowers them, plays to their strengths and is allied to their aspirations – not a dead end, dependency state;
- and it must encourage 'fraternity' – or social cohesion. It should help integrate society, not divide it.

The last point, the role of social security in promoting social cohesion, has been neglected in recent decades. It is timely therefore to remind ourselves how a generation of social reformers focussed on this objective.

The theme of social cohesion was certainly central to Beveridge's vision. As his biographer, José Harris, has observed[60], Beveridge had long believed, thirty years before his report, that social insurance was "a means not simply of meeting needs but of promoting social solidarity and of bringing institutions and individuals into partnership with the State". She observes that this theme was not only still powerfully present in the Beveridge Report "but now it was a cohesion that was ethical rather than organisational".

The foremost advocate of an integrationist, universal and solidarity model of social welfare remains Richard Titmuss. He argued his case, in part, on the grounds that developing services and benefits simply for poor people would result in 'poor services'. As he wrote:

> ...*an impression is sustained that poor people are a distinctly separate and permanent sector of the population, a class or a race or a caste apart.*[61]

Rather he argued that:

> *Universal services available without distinction of class, colour, sex or religion, can perform functions which foster and promote attitudes and behaviour directed towards the values of social solidarity, altruism, toleration and accountability.*[62]

These words of Richard Titmuss from the year 1972, ring out as a strong truth that should guide the Labour Party towards a new social welfare approach in the second decade of the 21st century.

How do we move from values, which plainly articulated seem abstract, to formulating policies? A valuable bridging concept is citizenship.

I learn a lot from my Croydon constituents. One conversation in particular stands out. An elderly gentleman told me that his political heroes were Churchill (whose picture was displayed proudly on his wall) and Ernest Bevin. My constituent's concern, strongly but gently put, was that the country today no longer had clear values to guide it; that there was no agreed set of 'rules'. He contrasted this with that earlier post war era when he was young, which saw the emergence of the modern welfare state. He instanced, in particular, National Insurance: "you paid your contributions when you had a job, you could receive benefits when in need". Today he felt there was no such clarity, not just in social security, but more generally.

## *Defining citizenship*

A leading contribution to post war debate was Professor T H Marshall's 1949 lecture on citizenship. In a key passage, he stated:

> *Citizenship is a status bestowed on those who are full members of a community. All who possess the status are equal with respect to the rights and duties with which the status is endowed.*[63]

Marshall, of course, formulated his ideas in the post war years when the first ever majority Labour Government was expanding the practical realities of citizenship through its construction of the modern welfare state. He distinguished three elements of citizenship: civil, political and social.

## *21st century citizens*

Today, citizenship remains a crucial and provocative concept for a range of modern questions. Over six decades on from Professor Marshall's lecture, we see a nation very different from that of the early post war period. In contrast to unity and solidarity, partly forged out of the battles against Hitler, there is today more individualism and also more diversity in our population in the wake of substantial immigration. There is also a decline in those institutions that created solidarity, whether large industries such as coalmines, steelworks and factories, or church and chapel, trade unions and mass political parties. So there is less shared interest and less shared history. And globalisation weakens ties between company and community, when shareholders' and people's interests point in different geographical directions. These factors challenge the reality of citizenship and therefore make it more important to foster.

## *Rights and responsibilities*

This raises a central issue for a democracy: what are the fundamental rights and responsibilities of citizens? The question of the balance between these two is the key test. Often, the debate is approached more narrowly – too narrowly. Depending on political persuasion, the emphasis is placed solely on responsibility or rights. British politics has been weakened by the Left's almost exclusive focus on rights in recent decades (in contrast to a more traditional and equal emphasis on duty, whether as a member of the friendly society, the union or the co-op), and also by the Right's equally narrow emphasis on duty, turning its back on an earlier 'one nation' tradition.

It is therefore the issue of rights and responsibilities – the balance between them, and the implications for the state and other institutions – that offers one of the most fruitful ways of advancing debate. To focus on either one without the other is crass, too narrow, merely partisan and, in practical terms, leads up a policy cul-de-sac. But a focus on both rights and responsibilities provides a useful entrée into, and a moral foundation stone for, some of the key policy questions that Britain faces today. These include employment, child maintenance, health care and family. It also provides a template for defining and evaluating outcomes.

## *Individual responsibility*

The concept of citizenship not only raises important issues about social rights and responsibilities. We also need to recognise that citizens may also be the leaders of powerful organisations in both the public and private sectors. Talk of responsibility is sometimes used as a stick to threaten the poor, but responsibility also focuses attention on some of the most powerful in the land. If responsibility is good enough for the poor, it is certainly good enough for the rich. The banking crisis, which has plunged Britain into near recession and austerity, has highlighted the amorality of the banking class in particular and the top 1% of Britain's wealthy in general. There can be no less apt soundbite than Osborne's "we are all in this together", coming at a time when the incomes and wealth of the richest are sky rocketing, while those of low income families, the unemployed and the so-called 'squeezed middle', are either in decline or stagnating.

The rich preach that workers should make wage sacrifices for the sake of the economy, but that they themselves must be free to accumulate more riches, also for the sake of the economy. The major crisis of responsibility is a crisis affecting the rich and nothing I say about our social security system should distract from this fact. The crucial relevance, however, is that if there is an absence of ethics and duty at the so called top of our society, it becomes more difficult to induce these values among our least privileged.

The responsible nation should be one that fosters a strong sense of responsibility in the country as a whole, whether in government itself, the private sector, communities, families or individuals. It recognises that we grow stronger if we respect mutual rights and responsibilities and if there is a strong egalitarian ethic that cherishes, but also holds to account, each and every citizen.

Britain at its best manifests many of these characteristics. The National Health Service, par excellence, is based on this ethic and understanding. Daily life in our cities, towns and villages witness numerous examples of responsibility. The service provided by hundreds of thousands of citizens in their role as councillors, school governors and volunteers is a testament to this strong ethic in practice.

Moreover, there is a huge silent majority of families, where parents quietly bring up their children well, a responsibility that no longer ends when the child is 15 or 16 but lasts so much longer. Millions of others, the so-called informal carers, provide service to those with disabilities and serious frailty, such as dementia, simply through love and a strong sense of duty. Given the strength of the demographic tide, with so many more citizens living into their 80s and 90s, there is certainly more care provided by the modern family than ever before in history. So much for the absurdity of the charge that we are a 'broken Britain'.

We need public understanding and support for the principles and the practice of a modern welfare state. All citizens, whether as taxpayers, family members or as pension or benefit recipients, need to have confidence in the underlying ethos and the 'rules of the game'. A confidence that welfare is not a burden, but rather a crucial foundation stone for a well-functioning social democracy.

## Public Confidence

Is this the case today? I don't think so, at least not entirely. Parts of the welfare state, of course, are massively supported, notably the NHS. Yet, as many of us found during the 2010 election campaign, there is much public disquiet about alleged benefit scroungers and the work shy and a perceptible unease that hard working citizens are taken for granted; that parents who responsibly plan for family building go to the back of the housing queue; and that to work on a low income earns you little extra above benefit levels.

A recent survey[64] found that, in answer to the question 'do you agree or disagree that "the government pays out too much in benefits; welfare levels overall should be reduced", the total agreeing was a massive 74% – more Tory voters, yes (94%) but including 59% of Labour voters. A further question concerned "scroungers": respondents were asked how many welfare claimants fit this description. 39% of the total said 'a significant minority', a further 22% suggested 'around half of all claimants'. [An additional 7% thought 'most welfare claimants', while 25% said 'a small minority'.] Again significant numbers of Labour voters thought that there were many scroungers in the system. Another survey finding found that as many as 69% agreed with the statement 'our welfare system has created a culture of dependency. People should take more responsibility for their own lives and families'.

Now, this is complex territory and not all public grievance can be taken at face value: there's a fair share of urban mythology and certainly misunderstanding [and exceptional cases, eg families living courtesy of Housing Benefit in millionaire mansions, gain currency and undermine public confidence]. But public anxiety does contain very strong grains of truth that need to be recognised and acted upon.

Indeed, some on the Left seek to belittle the size and significance of benefit abuse or, by comparing it with tax avoidance, speak of its relative insignificance. They doubtless assume that raising the question undermines public confidence, yet the reverse is the case. We avoid this issue at our peril. Abuse is clear, certainly to many living on our estates and in poorer communities. Side-stepping benefit abuse is a grave disservice to legitimate public anger about the failure of some to comply with the duties that must accompany rights, if the system is to be perceived as fair. Fraud is difficult to quantify but the fact is that fraud costs £1.32 billions, some 0.8% of total benefit expenditure[65]. A further £1.3 billion loss was due to customer error. For tax credits, fraud is estimated at £400 millions[66]. The scale of abuse was clear to me when I had Ministerial responsibility at the Department for Work & Pensions for tackling the problem [Regularly our anti-fraud officers would detect single parents who, in fact, live with boyfriends, the "incapacitated" out jogging or working on roofs, although the woman claiming benefit, because of an apparent inability to dress herself, who worked as a striptease artist was no doubt atypical.]

## 'Rights'

My argument is that a benefits system based on 'rights' alone is a system built on sand, rather than the granite rocks of citizenship, reciprocity and conditionality. It is one reason why we are losing the battle of public opinion on social security.

## *MOVING FORWARD: THE KEY BUILDING BLOCKS*

If we are serious about building a modern social security system fit for purpose in the 21st century, much detailed work will need to be done. Here, however, I suggest some of the key building blocks that are required. Some I discuss only briefly, but I will conclude by emphasising the importance of the contributory principle as a key building block.

### *Employment*

With the numbers of unemployed approaching three million, talk of the citizen's duty to work (whenever possible) may seem idealistic. It certainly emphasises the central need to place the attack on unemployment at the heart of national policy. Significantly the White Paper of 1944 on Employment Policy[67] accepted the Government's responsibility for the "maintenance of a high and stable level of employment". This is in sharp contrast to the Coalition Government's approach which seems to view rising unemployment as some kind of unfortunate, but inevitable, consequence of economic policy.

As noted earlier, Beveridge talked about the post-war challenge of attacking five giant evils. Critically, however, he emphasised the attack on unemployment:

> *Idleness is the largest and fiercest of the five giants and the most important to attack. If the giant Idleness can be destroyed, all the other aims of reconstruction come within reach. If not, they are out of reach in any serious sense and their formal achievement is futile.*[68]

Contemporary evidence, about the impact of unemployment on health, not to mention poverty, educational attainment, squalor and access to decent housing, illustrate all too graphically the modern resonance of Beveridge's warning . The challenge therefore is to place employment centre stage with strong implications for macro-economic policy but also for industrial policy (witness the Bombardier episode) and for skills and innovation. I believe that the urgent priority is to guarantee a job or training for Britain's school leavers. Few things can be more disheartening than leaving school and ending up in a wilderness of inactivity. This will require a national effort: the public sector and large businesses – Sainsbury's, Marks and Spencer's, construction companies and others, must be signed up to help achieve this objective.

*Skills and Education*

High levels of unemployment are not simply a consequence of today's austerity regime but have been a feature of the labour market in recent decades [Graph 1]. There is no consistent data going back to the immediate post-war period, but the evidence we have shows low unemployment following the war (census figures suggesting it was a little over 2% or so). Unemployment then increased with a peak in the 1970s and higher peaks in the 1980s, the 1990s and today. Similar trends apply to youth unemployment, albeit at a relatively higher rate than for all ages [Graph 2].

My own constituency experience in Croydon North reflects this data in human terms. Even during the 'boom' Labour years, many of my constituents remained unemployed. Yet there were vacancies and many migrants, typically from Eastern Europe, were easily finding jobs. How do we explain this seeming paradox? Explanations relate to job readiness, a lack of willingness to go the extra mile in search of work, and a frank lack of education and skills.

In contrast to the immediate years after the war, there are now far fewer jobs which require only low skills and more and more jobs that require high levels of literacy and numeracy at the very least, and often

**Graph 1**[69]

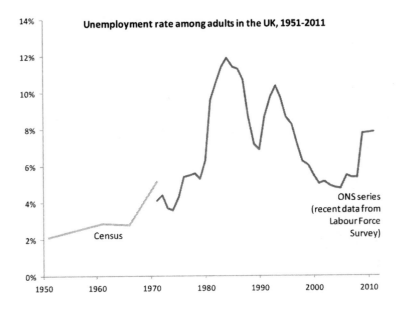

Unemployment rate among adults in the UK, 1951-2011

Census

ONS series
(recent data from
Labour Force
Survey)

sophisticated information technology skills and further and higher education qualifications. The last Labour government did much to address this problem, from literacy hours in our primary schools, tough targets at secondary level and a rising number entering university. But there is so much more to be done and we need to make a reality of 'lifelong learning' and a new programme to focus on those who lack skills.

*Strong Families*

There is no more crucial building block for 'social security' than the strong family. It is the family that brings home the lion's share of

**Graph 2[70]**

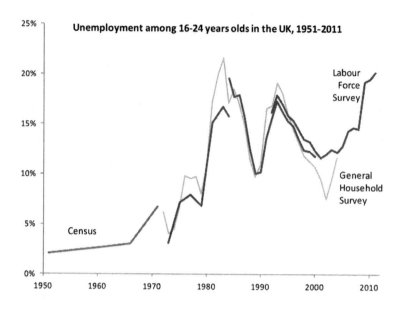

Unemployment among 16-24 years olds in the UK, 1951-2011

household income. There is a huge silent majority of families that bring up their children very well. Parents often play as important a role as the school in encouraging learning, from the bedtime story, to the dreaded question for children, 'have you done your homework?', from coaxing through stressful exams to often expensive parental support for further and higher education.

Our aim in family policy should be to be on the side of what I have called 'strong families'. Such families are to be found among many different kinds of households including those headed up by married couples, by those who are cohabiting and by single parents. We should play to their strengths and promote the right balance between rights and duties. We should be on the side of aspiration and ambition. It should be a positive family policy, but therefore one that does not shy away from tough and controversial questions.

Yet, the family has undergone extensive changes since the 1940s and some of these present challenges to both parliament and government.

The Right have their own family problems (a married tax allowance in the age of cohabitation!), but my task is to focus on the Left. From its early days, the last Labour Government faced internal tension between those who were thought to favour traditional family values and structures and those who sought to champion family diversity and in particular the needs of single parent families. Such a generalisation is partially unfair to both sides, but it will do as a generalisation! I think this tension resulted in a stand off: the Labour government failed to develop a coherent family policy. This is complex and dangerous terrain, not least because politicians are human beings too, often fallible ones. Alongside the rest of the population, they include the separated and divorced, they make their own personal mistakes and their own children may run into difficulty. The personal can become political, as an intrusive media are quick to point out. Many politicians shy away from this terrain.

Labour was hardly inactive, however, and many of our policies helped the family, from child trust funds to sure start centres, but I think we failed to tackle some fundamental and very difficult questions.

There is always the danger of being sanguine about the past when it comes to families and children, looking for that golden age that never existed. There are, however, serious questions about the welfare of some children and the consequent impact of dysfunctional families on communities. A revolution affecting family life in Britain has created a diversity of family forms and it is not a bloodless revolution.

- Why are Britain's divorce rates among the highest in the world?
- Why do we have such a high percentage of single (never married) families?
- Why do so many fathers effectively abandon their own children, certainly financially, but often in other respects too?

One consequence of such trends is that the welfare state, and therefore taxpayers and, therefore other parents, have had to take on financial burdens that properly should fall to the families themselves.

Let me ask a question? Of all the children living in separated families, how many are financially supported by the 'absent' parent – normally the father? Answer: only one half[71]. Other data from DWP[72] for all separated families, totalling 2.5 million, shows that there is a Child Support Agency (CSA) payment liability or non-CSA arrangement in place for some 1.51 million. It is important to note, however, that this does not mean, in all cases, that payments are actually made or that they are made in full.

Child support, as evidenced by the experience that Britain, the USA, Australia and other countries demonstrates, is complex and extremely controversial territory. [My only law of politics that I have formulated is that some things are difficult because they are difficult!] Both Conservative and Labour governments have tried to get this one right, but with only partial success. While absent parents working in the public services, or for many companies, pay their maintenance regularly, because they are easy to track down, many others escape the system, through self employment and other means. This is social policy at its most challenging – an attempt by the state, on behalf of children and the wider community, to get maintenance payments when individuals are at their most raw and angry, following a painful separation, often exacerbated by conflicts over child access.

The depressing picture of irresponsibility shown by the child support data is but one indicator of a far wider and disturbing demography. There are too many children being brought up in families which are uncaring and chaotic, where there is no father figure. [How many young people convicted in the recent riots had positive father role models?] Indeed there are some families where men, casual boyfriend figures, pass through families and sometimes abuse children. As recent grim cases remind us, children are more likely to be murdered in these family circumstances than by strangers. There are also many more children who are the victims of family breakdown, the often unseen victims of mothers and fathers at war with one another. This is an inconvenient truth about the social revolution that has engulfed many families.

Some of these children will face harmful impacts on their socialisation, their educational attainment and consequently their future life chances. The last Labour government did much. However, there is a need for some fresh thinking. First, we must emphasise that the frontline of defence against insecure childhoods must be the promotion of the strong family. How do we achieve this? And how do we ensure that social and benefit programmes nurture and support, rather than discourage, responsible parents? Second, we must ensure that public expenditure is used to most effect, pooling portions of departmental budgets in pursuit of agreed priorities, such as investing in early intervention, raising teenagers' aspirations and promoting parental responsibility. Spending money effectively requires a strong focus on objectives, not dull allegiance to Whitehall configuration.

## A 21ST CENTURY SOCIAL INSURANCE STRATEGY

A final, but substantial, building block for a modern social security system is my major theme – the renaissance and modernisation of the contributory principle, one based by definition on a proper balance between rights and duties. The idea of life cycle accounts is worth exploring. These might include the following characteristics. First, they would be individualised accounts, accessible via the internet. Individuals should have a sense of 'ownership' of the account. Second, there should be flexibility, including the ability to access money at certain, albeit limited, points in one's life cycle, ahead of retirement. The ability to 'borrow' certain amounts against future contributions should also be a feature. [I do not under-estimate the need to build up funds for a decent pension, but the ability to draw on social insurance for specific purposes pre-retirement is attractive.] Third, the scheme should enable individuals to make payments into their own account. This would be a welcome feature, not least at a time when many commercial schemes resemble a confusing savings swindle. What should a new social insurance system cover? What 21st Century life cycle risks and circumstances might be included in a modern social insurance scheme?

## Unemployment

The current coverage of National Insurance is the starting point, but surely we can do better for the major risk of unemployment. Many of those who might subscribe to a popular perception that benefit levels are too high are shocked when they come face to face with the actualité of unemployment, as many are now doing. Unemployment insurance now lasts only six months; after that, if their partner is in work, there might be no Jobseekers' Allowance at all. Rates are very low: for the under-25s the benefit is just £56.25; for the over-25s it is £71 a week.

But more realistic unemployment benefit rates must rest on two things: a tougher stance on the duty to work and locating the goal of full employment at the heart of public policy.

## Pensions

As for National Insurance pensions, why should not individuals be enabled to make extra contributions into the system in exchange for guaranteed enhanced benefits? Given the low administrative costs of National Insurance, the system could offer a far better deal than those currently available from expensive private pension schemes, typically defined contribution schemes with low annuity rates.

## *Child Endowment*

Life cycle accounts should include the reincarnation of child trust funds, not least to inculcate the savings habit early. A new child endowment should be vested in favour of every child at birth. There would be strict rules about the use of such an endowment. These might include the funding of post-16 or later further education, a deposit for home ownership, etc.

How would it be funded? The current period of austerity, that has affected families so badly, was caused primarily by the banking crisis, when government was forced to nationalise large segments of the banking system. When the nationalised shares are finally sold (and this should not be done at a low price) we should think more imaginatively than merely returning the money to the Treasury for general usage. What better than to use some of this capital to invest in our children's future through the new endowment scheme? This would indicate that we take our newest citizens seriously and seek to promote their futures. Another mechanism would be to enable the funding of the new child endowment scheme through loans against future National Insurance contributions.

## *Childcare*

Ideally a new social insurance scheme should recognise the changing patterns of care within the nuclear and extended family, in the light of increasing women's (and mothers') employment and the care crisis posed by an ageing population. These represent challenges which were not present in the society that Beveridge experienced. Should a modernised social security system, possibly through social insurance, include either a childcare payment or enhanced parental leave (to be shared by both father and mother)?

## Long term care

While Beveridge has much to say about pensions, surely today he would also have emphasised frailty in old age and the burden of long-term care as one of the important risks to be covered by social insurance. The Dilnot Commission[73] has made important recommendations in this area, essentially proposing a sharing of costs between the individual and the State. Is there scope for a new insurance contract that would help meet these costs?

100 years after the introduction of National Insurance, and indeed 70 years after the publication of the pioneering Beveridge report, it is time for fresh thinking about the role that social insurance might play in our national social security system. This is not about history or nostalgia, but rather the search for a system of social security that commands public respect (and must therefore follow public consultation and debate) and one based on sound public finance. A hotch-potch of benefit provision, based on neither clear values nor public consensus, will fail to see us through in the difficult years that lie ahead. A new social contract between citizen and state, based on clear rights and duties, is the way forward.

*This lecture was delivered to an invited audience at the House of Commons on 24th April 2012.*

# 3.

# *Values*

*1) Labour values – past, present and future*

---

**February 1937, Highbury, London**

After an evening's canvassing, my father and two other young people
stand on a cold Islington street corner and sing:

*So raise the scarlet standard high,*
*Within its shade we'll live and die,*
*Though cowards flinch and traitors sneer,*
*We'll keep the Red Flag flying here!*

Labour's anthem duly sung, goodbyes are said…

---

My father, Arthur Wicks, was a committed socialist (and pacifist) and
a good public servant in his beloved Islington and Hackney. His
principles and values were forged during his working class
upbringing in North London. He joined the Labour Party at an early
age in the 1930s and, from all I know of those years, I can easily
understand his motivation. Born after the Second World War, I
followed in his footsteps and was influenced by him in so many
different ways. But I also benefitted from post-war opportunities that
were denied to those, like him, who left school at 14. I attended first

a polytechnic and then a university to study political and social science.

So while Arthur Wicks' early years were working class, mine by any objective standard, were comfortably middle-class[74]. He was born in 1915, and his childhood and life were shaped by parents who were born in the 1880s. I was born three decades later. My own children should live into the second half of the 21$^{st}$ century and my grandchildren, or at least some of them, might help to celebrate the dawning of a new century.

My point in mentioning these brief family details is not, on this occasion, autobiographical, but political. My father's political motivations and instincts can be easily understood. But why, in the 21st century, should his successors – young men and young women – become 'political'? And if they do so, why should they be on the left – progressives, radicals, socialists or social democrats? Why not simply 'live the life' and enjoy the fruits of a still affluent society? Why not simply focus on career, personal development goals, travel and personal relationships while, no doubt, doing some good here and there and occasionally 'putting something back'?

It was the great American economist John Kenneth Galbraith who so aptly characterised the potentially de-sensitising effects of prosperity and attractions of being able to lead a comfortable life without feeling obliged to worry too much about social justice. As he wrote in 1958:

*These are the days when men of all social disciplines and all political faiths seek the comfortable and the accepted; when the man of controversy is looked upon as a disturbing influence; when originality is taken to be a mark of instability; and when, in minor modification of the scriptural parable, the bland lead the bland[75].*

But, as he added more than 30 years later in his book *The Culture of Contentment,* a political system consecrated to the needs of a growing and self-absorbed middle class risks sowing the seeds of unrest if it ignores the needs of the poorest in society[76].

No one would deny that as society has changed, so the Labour Party has needed to change and adapt its message to altered priorities. But it is well worth asking the simple question: 'What are we about?' What is it that Labour, in the second decade of the 21<sup>st</sup> century, stands for?

This is plainly not a question that much troubled many of our founders. They viewed Labour's purpose as striving to improve the lot of the great majority, the working class. It was a struggle against the consequences of economic depression, unemployment and the dole; and it was a campaign for jobs and fairly shared prosperity. It was about the need for decent standards and services. Labour's origins were a cry against poverty and inequality and for a better society in a better world.

Despite its overwhelmingly practical purpose, the Labour Party has scarcely been unaffected by theory and philosophy. Fabian Society members were particularly influential in its early years, not least Beatrice and Stanley Webb who wrote its original constitution. A host of writers and thinkers, from the economist and political theorist G. D. H. Cole through to the economic historian R.H. Tawney and, later, the economist, Member of Parliament and Minister, Anthony Crosland, were influential. Yet practical concerns for achieving practical outcomes have predominated. For Herbert Morrison, Home Secretary in Clement Attlee's post-War Government, the definition of socialism was clear. It was, he said:

*What the Labour Government does*

This was, after all, a less cynical age. Party supporters, not least a growing number of local councillors like my father, got on with the practical business of building houses and schools, opening parks and swimming pools, improving public health and removing slums.

Today things may not seem overwhelmingly different in the sense that practical matters still swarm into focus if we are asked to describe our Party's purpose. Protecting the National Health Service, raising educational attainment, creating employment, tackling crime and anti-social behaviour, creating apprenticeships, making international aid available and a hundred other things come to mind. Yet a century and more after the founding of the Labour Party, we witness a very different society and economy from that of the late 19th century. Heavy manufacturing and the industries that fed it – textiles, steel and coal, for example – have been supplanted by massive growth in the service sectors and a revolution in science and communications.

There is a different social structure, with the middle classes now the majority, rather than the working class. Changing demography has created longer and more complex life cycles, resulting in an ageing population and the emergence of more varied family structures. When the Labour Party was finding its feet in the early 20th century, the major health challenges were the fight against conditions such as diphtheria and tuberculosis, highlighting the importance of the public health movement. Today, innovations in scientific research open the way to new advances; for example the use of stem cell research to conquer conditions like cancer and heart disease that continue to debilitate humankind. Far from impeding change, Labour's rise to political maturity has fostered many of the most positive improvements in our society, from the National Health Service and the welfare state, to employment rights, fair rents, wider access to higher education and the elimination of slum housing.

In the past 20 years too, British society has increasingly felt the impact and growth of a globalised economy. There have been benefits, through free trade, but there have also been pitfalls. We scarcely need reminding about the consequences of the banking crisis in 2008 and the economic malaise that has followed. The preceding years of rising prosperity, meanwhile, appear to have brought about changes in attitudes and the psychology of the nation, with an apparent increase in materialism and individualism. Social solidarity has, by the same token, been undermined. There is widespread agreement that Britain has become a less cohesive society; although opinions about the causes

– from the idolisation of market forces to the loss of neighbourly communities and mass immigration – vary widely[77].

What does Labour have to offer this evolving society? If Labour's purpose seemed clear in the 1900s, and very clear in the 1940s, what is it in the 2010s? The advent of 'New Labour' in the 1990s included a strong assertion that while Labour's traditional values held true, the task was to apply them in changing times. As John Prescott phrased it memorably (and often): "Traditional values in a modern setting."[78]

Any political party seeking electoral success needs to reflect and reassess at critical periods in its history. For parties of the right this can entail, at best, a truly radical reappraisal of basic positions. Witness the Tory Party's 19th century collision with the emerging democracy and its slow embrace of the mass franchise. Take also the intellectual journey of Conservatives, from Benjamin Disraeli to Harold Macmillan, in coming to terms with poverty and the emergence of a welfare state. Thatcherism produced, for a time, a partially successful counter-revolution: witness Sir Keith Joseph's telling observation in 1976 that "…it is clear that the middle ground was not a secure base but a slippery base to socialism and state control." In that context, David Cameron's move, while in opposition, towards more central territory still seems more of an exercise in style rather than substance. Indeed, the Coalition is now retrenching public services, using the public deficit as an all too convenient excuse, and driven by a rampant right-wing (the equivalent of America's libertarian, anti-government Tea Party) rather than the 'one nation' Conservatism of Disraeli and Macmillan.

For the left, and for the Labour Party in particular, soul-searching has been a more than periodic requirement. A continuous debate between left and right, has been inevitable – and welcome; as it is in any 'broad church' party political system of the kind we have in Britain.

Landmark episodes stand out: notably Tony Crosland's exercise in revisionism, *The Future of Socialism*[79] and, more recently, Tony Blair's 1990s re-branding of the Party as 'New Labour'. The former argued against too narrow a focus on public ownership – famously enshrined in Clause IV Section 4 of the Party's then constitution – in favour of the broader goal of achieving social justice. The latter succeeded in replacing the traditional commitment to nationalisation with a wider assertion of Labour's democratic socialist aims. In the current words of the *Labour Party Rule Book*:

> *It believes that by the strength of our common endeavour we achieve more than we achieve alone, so as to create for each of us the means to realise our true potential and for all of us a community in which power, wealth and opportunity are in the hands of the many, not the few, where the rights we enjoy reflect the duties we owe, and where we live together, freely, in a spirit of solidarity, tolerance and respect.*

The political analyses of Crosland in the 1950s and Blair in the 1990s were different in many respects. But they surely had a number of fundamental things in common. These can be summarised as: a need to distinguish between ends and means; a recognition that basic values remain true and enduring; and an understanding that changing times demand the adjustment of policies and prescriptions to present day and likely future realities and requirements. They both sought to re-assess the dynamic between capitalism and socialism; and therefore, the relationship between the market and the state. And that process – as we confront the great issues of our own time, from the banking crisis to global warming – must now go on.

After 13 years in power, and following its 2010 defeat, there is a need for Labour to reappraise where we stand; where we need to be, if the Party is to maintain its relevance to British people and their concerns, fears and aspirations. This is not least because some (though not all) 'New Labour' positions have become almost fossilised into an ideology that involves an uncritical embrace of market dogmas: a kind of 'market good', 'public sector bad' mentality. Sadly, at times, this has resulted in rhetoric that seems to embrace riches and vulgar wealth almost as a deliberate insult to Labour's basic values of equality (and perhaps as a signal that New Labour now truly believes in the values of capitalism)[80]. But while some might see the debate as a further disagreement between the Labour traditionalists and the would-be 'ultra-Blairites', my argument is that none of this factionalism will do. Rather we need to assess on the rock of basic values, some key questions for radicals.

*So what are we really about?*

To throw the discussion forward, let us slightly re-phrase my earlier question and ask what are we in the 21st Century Labour Party *really* about? What are our end purposes and underlying values? It gets complex (increasingly so) but it starts out simply. We can see that society, left in a raw state, would be harsh at best, and cruel and vicious at worst. The powerful would rule unfettered, and the poor would be powerless. The purpose of democracy and politics – certainly radical politics – is to challenge this supposedly 'natural' order. That is why, by no coincidence, it is nearly always the right wing in politics that can be found calling for 'less government'. The left is about taming, civilising and democratising the economic order. It is about a set of values that cherish every individual, but seek to enhance community and the collective.

That's the simple bit. It gets more complicated when we attempt to put more philosophical flesh on these ideas, and more complex still when we seek to fashion policy instruments that are relevant to current and future trends, and changing power structures – not least the challenge of globalisation and radically shifting job patterns around the world. How can we continue to pursue compassion and conscience in the midst of such affluence and inequality as we witness today?

*Moral values*

As previously observed, the Labour Party has not been inspired by any one tradition, philosophical school or set of beliefs. Rather it derives its ideas and experience from a range of historical strands. Some are drawn from other parts of the world, but the Labour tradition is firmly British in character. Democratic socialism is a practical manifestation of centuries of radical struggle and working-class desire for a better society. Tony Benn is just one among a number of Labour politicians who have noted the British labour movement draws its inspiration from a history that goes back over many centuries. Christianity and secularists, the Levellers, the Chartist campaign for Parliamentary democracy, trade unionism, feminism, Marxism and other radical and liberal ideas, ideals and campaigns have all influenced socialist thought and action[81].

However, these rich origins can make for confusion and certainly do not point in one clear direction. Crosland, in his brief review of the traditions of British socialism, concluded in part that there are some fundamental differences between different schools of socialist thought and that the doctrines are often mutually inconsistent. For example, Fabian collectivism and welfare statism require a view of the state that is diametrically opposed to a Marxist view. The syndicalist tradition is anti-collectivist. The Marxist tradition is anti-reformist. Owenism[82] differs fundamentally from Marxism and syndicalism on the class war. Morrisite communes and socialist guilds are incompatible with nationalisation... and so on[83]. Crosland does, however, note that:

> *The single one element common to all the schools of thought has been the basic aspirations, the underlying moral values. It follows that these embody the only logically and historically permissible meaning of the word 'socialism'.*

A good broad starting point for the moral values that underpin Labour's tradition of democratic socialism is the definition provided by William Morris, in 1896:

> *What I mean by Socialism is a condition of society in which there should be neither rich nor poor, neither master nor master's man, neither idle nor overworked, neither brain-sick brainworkers, nor heart-sick handworkers, in a world, in which all men would be living in equality of condition, and would manage their affairs unwastefully, and with the full consciousness that harm to one would mean harm to all – the realization at last of the meaning of the word commonwealth.*[84]

This late 19th century definition is interesting in that it not only highlights equality, but also emphasises, translated into modern parlance, environmental sustainability ("manage their affairs unwastefully") while also asserting the value of non-economic objectives ("neither brain-sick brainworkers").

## Equality (and re-distribution)

As British politics in the past 20 years has amply demonstrated, politicians, pundits and philosophers, when confronted by an ideological dichotomy (such as that between 'capitalism' and 'socialism'), often reach out for new insights that they optimistically label their 'Big Idea' or 'Third Way'. Faced with this, I like the sharp observation made by A. H. "Chelly" Halsey, at a time in the 1990s when talk of 'stakeholding' was in vogue, that there really have not been any new ideas since the French Revolution – and the celebrated trilogy of 'Liberty', 'Equality' and 'Fraternity'. A passionate belief in equality was certainly central to William Morris's definition of democratic socialism. He believed it fundamental that all citizens should be born with equal rights, and that they should give and receive respect from others. He expected that they should contribute their best to society; taking on a fair share of responsibility according to their abilities and receiving a fair and equal share in the distribution of resources. This socialist belief in 'equality' is, it seems to me, substantially different from the emphasis that conservatives and liberals place on *equality of opportunity* (which is akin to the belief that underpins the capitalist-inspired 'American dream'). For as R. H. Tawney noted:

*Nothing could be more remote from Socialist ideals than the competitive scramble of a society which pays lip service to equality, but too often means by it merely equal opportunities of becoming unequal.* [85]

But how much equality? This is a crucial question, though one that is often avoided; not least because it raises difficult questions. In particular, while it is easy to demonstrate, from a socialist perspective – or indeed any ethical standpoint – that the current distribution of income, wealth, resources and opportunity is based on *no* rational criteria (why should a hedge fund analyst earn more than a nurse, or a city stockbroker more than a steelworker?), it is harder to determine what an equitable distribution of income should be. The true egalitarian, of course, would argue like Marx for a distribution of resources 'from each according to his or her ability, to each according to his or her need'. This remains a worthy objective, but a programme for five years in government needs to be based on more humble, albeit radical, objectives! There has to be a national debate about income; or at least the start of one. And while few would accept today a completely equal distribution of resources, I remain convinced that there is a majority constituency to be won in favour of a much fairer distribution.

The principle advanced by the American philosopher John Rawls in the 1970s of 'justice as fairness' is helpful here. This philosophical construct supposes that individuals in a society are able to choose which arrangements for their society would be just, without knowing where they, themselves, would be placed within the society. A 'veil of ignorance' operates. Rawls argues that people in these circumstances would choose two rather different principles. The first requires equality in the assignment of basic rights and duties. The second holds that social and economic inequalities (for example inequalities of wealth and affluence) are only acceptably just if they result in compensating benefits for everyone, and in particular for the least advantaged members of society.[86] This, of course, is a philosophical exercise based on a theoretical premise. But it is not without contemporary relevance, when many workers exist on very basic remuneration, while others on 'middle' incomes see little real increases in their incomes and a privileged few are able to award themselves huge gains in income and capital.

[MW indicated here that he planned to add further material about competing definitions of equality.]


## Liberty (and human rights)

All modern political parties claim 'liberty' as their own, so does anything distinguish Labour's embrace of liberty from anyone else's? I think it does. One of the great ironies of modern politics has been the ability of conservatives, of whatever party, to portray themselves as the champions of liberty. Moreover, they have been allowed, with remarkably little challenge, to contrast liberty with equality, arguing that the two are incompatible and that equality will inevitably deny liberty and freedom.

So let us ask ourselves what great freedoms does the modern conservative care most about. Do they emphasise the freedom for babies to survive and thrive in spite of adverse social conditions? Do they favour the freedom of the young to get jobs, whatever their class or colour? Or maybe the freedom for old people to live out their lives in decent housing and not to die from the cold when bitter weather strikes? Of course not. Nothing could be further from their minds: as their own priorities and actions, when in government, demonstrate. Rather they define 'liberty' and 'freedom' so narrowly that they become mere labels to justify their own privileges and bloated life styles. Can it be coincidence that such terms are employed most passionately and consistently by the rich to defend their 'rights' to buy privileged education and medical care for themselves and their families, heedless of the consequences for the rest of society?

This has always been the case. Throughout our history, and stretching back at least 200 years, Conservatives and other defenders of the status quo have opposed reform, whether it has been concerned with factory conditions, taxation, education or health, on the spurious grounds that they somehow infringe liberty and freedom. During the 1945 general election campaign, Winston Churchill, in his first radio broadcast, charged that a socialist policy was abhorrent to British ideas of freedom. Clement Attlee, replied in the strongest terms:

> *I entirely agree that people should have the greatest freedom compatible with the freedom of others. There was a time when employers were free to work little children for 16 hours a day. I remember when employers were free to employ sweated women workers on finishing trousers at a halfpenny a pair. There was a time when people were free to neglect sanitation so that thousands died of preventable diseases. For years every attempt to remedy these crying evils were blocked by the same plea of freedom for the individual. It was in fact freedom for the rich and slavery for the poor.*[87]

R.H Tawney also memorably warned against the Tory understanding of liberty:

> *It is a doctrine of liberty which is disposed to regard it as involving, not action to enlarge opportunities and raise individual faculty to the highest possible level, but guarantees for the continued enjoyment by*

*fortunate individuals and groups of such powers and advantages as past history and present social order may happen to have conferred on them.*[88]

More than half a century later we can expect to see this time-honoured Tory tradition continue: the misappropriation of the most inspiring words in the English vocabulary in defence of the most obscene privilege.

In approaching these questions, I suggest that socialists should not merely be guided by utilitarian principles – as in seeking 'the greatest happiness of the greatest number'. They should be inspired by a strong conviction that equality is not so much a goal in itself – which might mean merely the equality of drab uniformity – but the key means of promoting liberty and fraternity. Restricting the freedom of a small minority can, on that basis, be justified; but only when it is clear and demonstrable that this will lead to greater freedom for the majority. Action when doing this must always be guided by the principles of welfare and justice, and never by spite or anger.

[MW's notes show that he planned to include further discussion on the association between liberty and human dignity, and on the extent that restrictions on liberty might be justified in the interests of public security (such as those imposed following terrorist attacks.)]

### *Fraternity (and social cohesion)*

The third value belonging to the revolutionary trilogy has received less attention than liberty and equality. It is seldom articulated today, certainly in its original form[89]. It remains, nevertheless, an important value – as French scholars, in particular, continue to testify. Modern interpreters of its continuing significance have suggested, variously, that it was the 'heart and soul' of the original revolutionary trinity, or that the role of fraternity is to reconcile liberty and equality[90]. Some writers have also talked about a gradual convergence between the words 'fraternity' and 'solidarity'. As a guiding value 'fraternity' focuses our attention on the society that we are all members of and provides an implied contrast with mere, naked individualism. It emphasises our common humanity, fellowship and shared collective interests with our fellow citizens.

Equality, considered in isolation, might merely be taken to mean some quest for dreary uniformity, or a mere arithmetical objective. Liberty, viewed narrowly, might be misunderstood as justification for the most selfish, egotistical kind of individualism. However, when the two are bound together with fraternity there is an immediate implication of our strong mutual ties to others, and a sharing of rights and responsibilities. The relevance of 'fraternity' today, and in future, requires its translation into the term 'solidarity', or perhaps even 'community'. We might note with some caution how these are terms that have been continually 'rediscovered' during recent decades, but they, nevertheless, carry a useful, modern-day resonance. They lead us directly, for example, towards modern-day concerns that society is not as cohesive as it once was and that the elusive material, known as 'social fabric', is somehow fraying – not only at the edges. They also plunge us into a debate as to why key social institutions are not as well supported as they were in the past. These – depending on the tastes and disposition of those engaged in the argument – variously include the church, trade unions, high street shops, political parties, public houses and polling stations (and the worrying tendency towards lower participation in elections).

Immigration is also an issue here; and one that, despite being much contested and controversial, has been less honestly addressed than it deserves. Some view mass immigration from the Indian subcontinent and West Indies, and more recently from Poland and other European Union accession states, as the creative force for a vibrant, multicultural society. But it is evident that others associate it with socio-economic tensions and a reduced sense of national identity and cohesiveness.

Much of the recent debate about 'community' has taken place through the lens of race and migration and it seems to me that this, regrettably, has often got in the way of a more comprehensive discussion about community itself. Other factors that are judged by some to have adversely affected community include improved mobility – for example, the ability to frequent out of town supermarkets and malls at the expense of the high street – and the advent of personal computers and computer gaming, militating against more obviously sociable behaviour. Yet much of this can be contested. For example, there may be fewer pubs than in the past, but the popularity of 'social media' does not suggest that people have ceased communicating with friends and others with whom they share a community of interest.

[MW's manuscript indicates that he intended to expand and develop this part of his argument.]

As already noted, the Labour Party throughout its history has been characterised by its practical approach to democratic socialism. It has never been much impressed by ideology for its own sake, and that is part of its attraction for many of us who are members. I myself would argue that without a requirement to move from principle to practice, from philosophy to policy, all talk of 'values' would simply be armchair mush. Yet it is also, surely, right that the banking and financial crises in which we are entangled should encourage us to reflect: not only on the kind of economy that Labour should seek to build post-crunch, but also on something wider and more important: the kind of society we wish to live in.

## 2) *Rights, responsibilities and the welfare state*

We are rightly proud of the Labour Government's achievements in social policy from 1997 to 2010: not least the reductions in unemployment that were achieved, the minimum wage, the introduction of Child Tax Credits, the creation of Sure Start for pre-school children and the enhancement of Child Benefit. We are, rightly, resolved to oppose as strongly as possible the Coalition Government's enthusiastic and tragic assault on the incomes and life chances of many millions of families, including vulnerable people and those with modest retirement incomes.

But Labour's position – our stance – cannot sensibly remain there. It is not our task simply to attempt to build barricades around the welfare state just as we left it circa 2010. The wider point worth repeating is that we must not fall into the trap of retreating into the comfort zone of opposition for its own sake. The Labour Government's policies were not the end of the story and they left vital, unfinished business. At the same time, new challenges are emerging, driven by significant demographic, family, and labour market trends. Public attitudes towards issues such as work–life balance are also changing, with many young fathers and mothers wanting more time with their children while maintaining their careers.

The starting point, as we seek to develop coherent and affordable policies for the future, must be our values. These are the underlying beliefs that shape our key principles and it seems to me that the welfare state is fertile territory for the articulation of our values and the policies that follow. I have written elsewhere (see above) about the extraordinary durability of the trinity of principles made famous by the French revolutionary battle cry of 'Liberty, Equality and Fraternity'. It seems to me that we must aim for a more equal society, but one that liberates individuals and families, empowers them, playing to their strengths and allied to their aspirations. We do not want a dead-end, dependency state. And we must seek to encourage fraternity – or, in more modern parlance, social cohesion. The state in 21st century Britain should help to integrate society, not divide it.

*Rights and responsibilities*

But how do we move from values which, even when plainly articulated, may continue to seem abstract, to formulating policies? A valuable bridging concept is citizenship and the balance that needs to be struck between rights and duties. The rights agenda enhances the citizen's liberty and also promotes equality, while duties recognise the obligation to fellow citizens and therefore to society as a whole. In this context, I have always thought that a key contribution to contemporary debate comes from the lecture on citizenship given in 1949 by the great pioneer of social science, T. H. Marshall. As the editors of one relatively recent volume of commemorative essays commented:

> *It was at once modest and powerful, relevant to the society of his day but with wide theoretical and social philosophical resonance.*[91]

In a key passage, Marshall argued that:

> *Citizenship is a status bestowed on those who are full members of a community. All who possess the status are equal with respect to the rights and duties with which the status is endowed.*[92]

He formulated his ideas in the early post-war years when the first-ever majority Labour government was expanding the practical realities of citizenship through its construction of the modern welfare state. Marshall, in particular, distinguished three elements of citizenship: civil, political and social. By the last he meant:

> *... the whole range from the right of a modicum of economic welfare and security to the right to share to the full in the social heritage and to live the life of a civilised being according to the standards prevailing in society.*[93]

He also noted that relevant institutions were the education system and the social services.

In my view, citizenship, and its interpretation in the 21$^{st}$ century, remains a crucial and provocative concept for a range of modern questions. It raises a key issue for a democracy: namely, what are the fundamental rights *and* responsibilities of citizens? The question of the balance between these two is a key test. Often, the debate is approached too narrowly. Depending on political persuasion, the emphasis is placed solely on responsibilities or solely on rights. British politics has been weakened by the left's almost exclusive focus on rights – at least in recent decades – and also by the right's equally narrow emphasis on duty; thereby turning its back on an earlier 'One Nation' tradition in the Tory Party.

Some nowadays argue that citizens should accept greater responsibilities for a whole spectrum of social and economic activities: for the misdemeanours of their children; for care of their elders; for filling gaps in the labour market; for crime prevention; and for much else besides. But they noticeably refrain from mentioning what rights citizens should expect in relation to any or all of these things. Others are too narrowly focused on demands for further rights; for example, to child care, to a decent income and to a job. These are perfectly good and reasonable things to want, but those who assert their entitlements rarely address the question of their own responsibilities in society.

It is, therefore, the issue of rights *and* responsibilities – including the balance between them and the implications for the state and other institutions – that offers one of the most fruitful ways of advancing the debate about welfare. To focus on one without the other is crass, too narrow, partisan and, in practical terms, leads us up a policy cul-de-sac. A focus on both rights and responsibilities provides a useful entrée into some of the key policy questions. However, the language of rights and responsibilities must not just be applied to the poor. To remain valid as a guiding principle, it must focus at least as much on the privileged and powerful.

We need to enhance the public's understanding and support for the principles and the practice of a modern welfare state and an appreciation of the balance between rights and responsibilities can help us to do just that. All citizens, whether as taxpayers, family members or as pension or benefit recipients, need to have confidence in the underlying ethos and the 'rules of the game'. They need to be confident that welfare is not a burden, but rather a crucial foundation stone for a well-functioning social democracy. However, I doubt if that is entirely the case today. Parts of the welfare state are massively supported, notably the NHS[94]. Yet, as many of us found during the 2010 election campaign, there is much public disquiet about alleged benefit scroungers and the work-shy and a perceptible unease that hard-working citizens are being taken for granted. It is not uncommon for people to believe that parents who responsibly plan for family building go to the back of the housing queue, or that to work on a low income earns you little extra above benefit levels. This is complex territory and not all public grievances can be taken at face value. A fair amount of urban mythology is involved and certainly misunderstanding. But public anxiety does contain some strong grains of truth that need to be recognised and acted upon.

## *Reviving the contributory principle*

One promising way in which we might set about bolstering public confidence in the fairness of benefits is, I think, by reviving the contributory principle. This was a major feature of the 1942 Beveridge Report which led to the substantial reforms enacted by Clement Attlee's post-war Labour government. As Beveridge put it:

> ...*social security must be achieved by co-operation between the State and the individual. The State should offer security for service and contribution.*

To which he added:

> ...*benefit in return for contributions, rather than free allowances from the State, is what the people of Britain desire.*[95]

In recent years, indeed decades, the contributory principle has been eroded. Nowadays both the public and, it has to be said, many politicians regard National Insurance contributions as simply another tax. It is noteworthy that the debate surrounding Labour's proposals for National Insurance contribution increases versus the Coalition decision to raise Value Added Tax to 20 per cent was all about taxation and economic impact. It was decidedly not about how this might relate to a well-understood system of social security. Hardly surprising, then, that many employees have long-since ceased to view their National Insurance contributions as something that confers rights and protection against the risk of poverty during periods of sickness or unemployment, and basic income security in old age.

The case for moving back towards a social insurance model and a renaissance of the contributory principle needs to be explored. As I have suggested, such a move would be underpinned by a principled view of citizenship and the mutual rights and responsibilities that it confers; including a duty to work when able to do so. It represents a practical response to the risks we face in our working lives and in old age. Not least among them is the risk that many will require long-term and expensive care in later life – and the need to insure against the costs. It also recognises the necessity of having a robust financial vehicle in place, capable of obtaining social insurance contributions from employees, their employers and the state.

Reviving the contributory principle, is I believe, an approach that would command public understanding and assent. There would, of course, be a continuing need for targeted, more selective policies to account for exceptional circumstances. But these, too, should be constructed on the foundation of social insurance and the contributory principle.

## 3) One planet

[MW planned to extend his discussion about political values in the 21$^{st}$ century to international issues, including climate change and global poverty and inequality. He drafted this opening paragraph.]

A sense of values, a sense of ethics, cannot stop at the White Cliffs of Dover, or any other national boundary. In essence the value base here is that, as humans living on the corner of Europe, we share our planet Earth with others. This includes parts of the globe that are our potential, past, or present enemies; and it certainly includes many countries and people who are much poorer than ourselves. Ethics – our values, and our duties – should not be defined or restricted by lines on maps. Not least, we need to have regard to our planet; this blue entity spinning around day by day. This is the Earth that we exploit and abuse and that, due to human existence, urbanisation and industrialisation, is now increasingly unhealthy, indeed sick. That this has happened is a consequence of many threats to the Earth's biodiversity, but mainly due to climate change.

# Malcolm Hunt Wicks – Chronology

| | |
|---|---|
| 1st July 1947 | Born at Brocket Hall, near Hatfield, Hertfordshire |
| 1952-1961 | Norfolk House School, Muswell Hill |
| 1961-1964 | Elizabeth College, Guernsey, Channel Islands |
| 1964-1965 | North West London Polytechnic |
| 1965-1968 | London School of Economics, BSc. Social Science |
| 7th Sept 1968 | Married Margaret Baron in Alderney, Channel Islands |
| 1968-1970 | Junior Fellow, Department of Social Administration, University of York |
| 1970-1972 | Researcher (Hypothermia), Centre for Environmental Studies |
| 1970-1974 | Lecturer in Social Administration, Department of Government Studies, Brunel University |
| 1974-1978 | Social Policy Analyst, Urban Deprivation Unit, Home Office |
| 1977-1978 | Lecturer in Social Policy, Civil Service College |
| 1978 | Author, *Old and Cold: hypothermia and social policy*, Heinemann |
| 1978-1983 | Research Director and Secretary, Study Commission on the Family |
| 1983 | Co-author, *Government and Urban Policy*, Blackwell |
| 1983-1992 | Director, Family Policy Studies Centre |
| 1985-1986 | Chairman, Croydon Labour Party Local Government Committee |
| 1987 | Author, *A Future for All: do we need a welfare state?* Penguin |
| 1986-1992 | Chairman, Winter Action on Cold Homes |
| 1992-1997 | Member of Parliament, Croydon North West |
| 1997-2012 | Member of Parliament, Croydon North |

| 1995 | Carers (Recognition and Services Act) 1995. A Private Member's Bill |
| 1998–1999 | Chair, House of Commons Education Select Committee |
| 1999–2001 | Parliamentary Under-Secretary for Lifelong Learning, Department for Education and Employment |
| 2001–2003 | Parliamentary Under-Secretary for Work, Department for Work and Pensions |
| 2003–2005 | Minister of State for Pensions, Department for Work and Pensions |
| 2005–2006 | Minister of State for Energy, Department of Trade and Industry |
| 2006–2007 | Minister of State for Science and Innovation, Department of Trade and Industry |
| 2007–2008 | Minister of State for Energy, Department for Business, Enterprise & Regulatory Reform |
| 2008–2010 | Prime Minister's Special Representative on International Energy Issues |
| 2008 | Appointed to the Privy Council |
| 2009 | Honorary Doctorate of Social Science, Brunel University |
| 2010–2012 | Chairman, National Grid Affordable Warmth Solutions |
| 2011 | Academician, Academy of Social Sciences |
| 2012 | Honorary Fellowship, Energy Institute |
| 29th September 2012 | Died at home in South Croydon, Surrey |
| December 2012 | Honorary Freeman, London Borough of Croydon (posthumous) |

# Notes

1    Now the Southern Housing Group.

2    Negretti and Zambra, optical and scientific instrument makers.

3    Lyons Tea Shops were as significant in the 1950s as, say, Starbucks is today. My mother would favour 'milk and a dash', which perhaps was that generation's latte – although served more quickly and cheaply.

4    John Redwood, Conservative MP for Wokingham since 1987 and Welsh Secretary from 1993-1995.

5    Aldermaston in Berkshire was home to the Government's Atomic Weapons Research Establishment.

6    In 1963-4 Nelson Mandela and nine other leaders of the African National Congress were put on trial by the apartheid regime, charged with promoting violent revolution and sabotage.

7    *The Freewheelin' Bob Dylan* (1963).

8    Michael Meacher, MP for Oldham West since 1970 and a Minister in the Wilson, Callaghan and Blair administrations.

9    Molly Meacher, a social worker and, since 2006, a cross-bench member of the House of Lords.

10    Jonathan Bradshaw, Professor of Social Policy at the University of York since 1981.

11    Heinemann, London.

12    This section draws on the paper *Benefit or burden? The objectives and impact of child support* by Melanie Henwood and Malcolm Wicks, (Family Policy Studies Centre, 1986).

13    Thinking back, there seems something desperately old-fashioned about the 'wallet to purse' controversy. Yet at the time it was clear that there were still many mothers who had no idea what their husbands earned and, therefore, whether the child tax allowance was benefiting their children.

I say 'old fashioned' though I am sure that today such inequality still exists in some families.

[14] House of Commons, 13 May 1975 vol 892 cc. 330-405.

[15] Under the Heath government this proposal emerged as a 'Family Income Supplement'.

[16] Frank Field, *Killing a Commitment: the cabinet v the children*, New Society, 17 June 1976.

[17] Frank Field, *Killing a Commitment: the cabinet v the children*, New Society, 17 June 1976.

[18] Frank Field, *Killing a Commitment: the cabinet v the children*, New Society, 17 June 1976.

[19] Frank Field, *Poverty & Politics*, Heinemann, 1982.

[20] Sir William Beveridge, *Social Insurance and Allied Services,* Cmd 6404, HMSO, 1942, para. 108.

[21] Melanie Henwood, Lesley Rimmer and Malcolm Wicks, *Inside the Family: changing roles of men and women*, Family Policy Studies Centre, October 1987 reprinted October 1992.

[22] Dame Margaret Beckett became Deputy Leader of the Labour Party in 1992 and, briefly, its interim Leader following the death of John Smith. She served in the Cabinet under Tony Blair and became Britain's first woman Foreign Secretary. She is now the longest-serving woman MP.

[23] Extract from Whitgift Archives, 21 December 1873.

[24] Robin Cook, Labour MP for Livingston from 1983 until his death in 2005. Foreign Secretary from 1997 – 2001 and Leader of the House of Commons from 2001–2003.

[25] The United Nations Protection Force in Bosnia Herzegovina and Croatia.

[26] Kate Hoey, MP for Vauxhall since 1989.

[27] Calum MacDonald, MP for the Western Isles, 1987-2005.

[28] I was interested to see that UNPROFOR had maintained a sense of humour in otherwise dismal circumstances: on the return trip to Zagreb, I noticed that my passport stamp read 'Maybe Airlines'.

[29] Mayday Hospital, now Croydon University Hospital.

30   The *Croydon Advertiser*, 22 October 1993.

31   Clare Short, MP for Birmingham Ladywood from 1983-2010. International Development Secretary in Tony Blair's Government from 1997-2003.

32   Henwood, M. & Wicks, M. (1984) *The Forgotten Army: Family Care and Elderly People.* London: Family Policy Studies Centre.

33   Secretaries of State (1989), Caring for People: Community care in the next decade and beyond, Cm 849, London: HMSO.

34   HC Deb 14 December 1994, Vol 251 c945.

35   HC Deb 3rd March 1995, Vol 255 cc1369-71.

36   HOL Deb 17 May 1995 Vol 564 c628.

37   Department of Health (1995), *Carers (Recognition and Services) Act 1995: Policy Guidance*, Paragraph 8, London: Department of Health.

38   Holzhausen E (1997), *In on the Act? Social Services' experience of the first year of the Carers Act*, London: Carers National Association.

39   The Care Bill published in May 2013 marked the latest stage in the evolution of policy on carers. It supported the proposals of the Law Commission to give carers new legal rights to support, and sought for the first time to put carers on an equal footing with those they care for.

40   Subsequently a West Yorkshire MP, Education Secretary under Gordon Brown and, after 2010, Shadow Chancellor.

41   Self-governing state schools, directly funded by central government, but with private sponsors. Introduced by the Labour Government (initially as 'City Academies') from 2000 onwards.

42   *Connexions*, piloted and introduced from 2000 onwards, created a 'one stop shop' for advice on education, training and careers for young people aged 13 to 19, including a network of personal advisers.

43   Anne Weinstock CBE, Chief Executive of the Connexions National Unit and subsequently Head of the Labour Government's Youth Task Force.

44   Claire Tyler, subsequently Director of the Labour Government's Social Exclusion Unit. Now the Liberal Democrat peer Baroness Tyler of Enfield.

45   Lord Sainsbury, Minister for Science and Innovation, 1997-2006.

46  It turned out that an efficient Eurostar attendant, Nadia, had found my phone when it started to ring. She must have been somewhat surprised to discover that 10 Downing Street was on the line, but her diligence ensured that the phone could be collected the next day. I like to imagine that Nadia, by dint of answering the Prime Minister's call, came close to being appointed Science Minister herself; I suspect she would have done a good job.

47  The use of electronic tracking to help monitor people with dementia who may be prone to wandering remains controversial. However, several schemes have been successfully piloted, and advances in technology are likely to lead to further application with improved acceptability of smaller devices, providing they are part of a package of support, rather than an impersonal alternative, and their use is subject to ethical guidelines.

48  Powell, E. (1977) *Joseph Chamberlain*. London: Thames & Hudson.

49  From Zeebrugge in Belgium to Bacton in Norfolk.

50  Malcolm Wicks MP (2009) *Energy Security: a national challenge in a changing world*. Department of Energy and Climate Change.

51  Parliamentary Under-Secretary of State, Department for Education & Employment; Parliamentary Under-Secretary of State, Department for Work & Pensions; Minister of State for Pensions, Department for Work & Pensions; Minister of State for Energy, Department of Trade & Industry; Minister of State for Science & Innovation, Department of Trade & Industry; Minister of State for Energy, Department for Business, Enterprise & Regulatory Reform.

52  D. Strahan, *The Last Oil Shock: A Survival Guide to the Imminent Extinction of Petroleum Man*, London, John Murray, 2007.

53  Department of Trade & Industry Energy Review Consultation Document, *Our Energy Challenge: Securing Clean, Affordable Energy for the Long-Term*, January 2006.

54  W S Churchill, *Liberalism and the Social Problem*, Hodder & Stoughton, 1909, p254.

55  Sir William Beveridge, *Social Insurance and Allied Services*, cmd 6404, HMSO, 1942.

[56] Sir William Beveridge, *Pillars of Security*, George Allen & Unwin, 1943, p42.

[57] Data are at Q2 (April–June) each year and are not seasonally adjusted.

[58] These households may contain individuals who are not family members. Couples include a small number of same-sex couples and civil partners.

[59] Dependent children are children living with their parent(s) aged under 16, or aged 16 to 18 in fulltime education, excluding all children who have a spouse, partner or child living in the household. These families may also contain non-dependent children.
*Source: Census, Labour Force Survey, Office for National Statistics.*

[60] José Harris, *William Beveridge: a biography*, Oxford University, 1997, p418.

[61] Keynote address given by Richard Titmuss at the XVIth International Conference on Social Welfare, The Hague, Netherlands, 1972, *Developing Social Policy in Conditions of Rapid Change*. 'Role of Social Welfare', published in *Welfare and Wellbeing, Richard Titmuss's contribution to social policy*, edited by Pete Alcock et al, The Policy Press, 2001.

[62] ibid.

[63] T H Marshall, *Citizenship and Social Class*, Cambridge University Press, 1950.

[64] Peter Kellner, *A Quiet Revolution*, Prospect, March 2012.

[65] House of Commons Library, based on Department for Work & Pensions benefits – fraud and error in 2010-11.

[66] House of Commons Library, based on HMRC Tax Credits – fraud and error in 2009-10.

[67] Employment Policy, cmd 6527, HMSO, 1944.

[68] Sir William Beveridge, 1942, op. cit.

[69] House of Commons Library, based on ONS series (recent data from Labour Force Survey).

[70] House of Commons Library, based on *Labour Force Survey* and *General Household Survey*.

[71] Minister for Disabled People, Maria Miller, Welfare Reform Debate, HC Deb 1 Feb 2012 vol 539 c909.

[72] DWP impact assessment on 'Strengthening families, promoting parental

responsibility: the future of child maintenance' consultation, Jan 2011 based on Internal Analysis using the DWP families with children population projection, 2008 *Families and Children Study* and September 2010 Child Support Agency administrative data.

73  Commission on Funding of Care and Support, *Fairer Funding for All*, chaired by Andrew Dilnot, July 2011.

74  My Islington Nan could not understand why, at the age of 16, I still had not got a job!

75  Galbraith, J.K. (1958) *The Affluent Society*. Boston: Houghton Mifflin.

76  Galbraith, J.K. (1992) *The Culture of Contentment*. Boston: Houghton Mifflin.

77  See, for example, Utting, D. (ed.) (2009) *Contemporary Social Evils*. Bristol: Policy Press/Joseph Rowntree Foundation.

78  To which he memorably once added: "Don't forget either part!"

79  Crosland, A. (1956) *The Future of Socialism*. London: Jonathan Cape.

80  Prominent New Labour 'rude boys' have of late been heard sticking two fingers up to some very basic social values.

81  Benn, A, (1980) *Arguments for Socialism*. Harmondsworth: Penguin.

82  Based on the views of the industrialist, philanthropist and social reformer Robert Owen (1771-1858).

83  Crosland, A. (1956) *The Future of Socialism*. London: Jonathan Cape.

84  Morris, W. (1896) *How I Became a Socialist*. London: Twentieth Century Press.

85  Tawney, R. H. (1966) 'The Radical Tradition'. In R. Hinden (ed.) *Twelve essays on politics, education and literature*, Harmondsworth: Penguin.

86  Rawls, J. (1971) *A Theory of Justice*. Cambridge MA: Belknap.

87  Attlee, C. (1954) *As It Happened*. London: Heinemann Educational Books.

88  Tawney, R.H. (1945) 'We Mean Freedom'. In C. Latham et al. *What Labour Could Do*. London: G. Routledge & Sons.

89  Perhaps because an avowal of 'brotherhood' seems out of kilter with gender equality in a feminist era.

90  See, for example, Ozouf, M. (1996) 'Liberty, Equality, Fraternity'. In P. Nora & L.D. Kritzman (eds.) *Realms of Memory: The Construction of the French Past (Vol. 1)*. New York: Columbia University Press.

91  Bulmer, M. and Rees, A. M. (1996) 'Conclusion: citizenship in the twenty-

first century'. In M. Bulmer, & A. M. Rees (eds.) *Citizenship today: the contemporary relevance of T.H. Marshall*. London: UCL Press.

92   Marshall, T. H. (1950) *Citizenship and social class and other essays*. Cambridge: Cambridge University Press.

93   Marshall, T.H. (1950) as above.

94   See, for example, Park, A. et al. (eds.) (2011) *British Social Attitudes 28*. London: NatCen / Sage. [See also Park, A. et al (eds.) (2012) *British Social Attitudes 29*. London: NatCen].

95   Beveridge, Sir W. (1942) *Social Insurance and Allied Services*. Cmd 6404. London: HMSO.

# Index